Bread

A Collection of Spiritual and Philosophical Essays

Francis J. Shaw

Copyright © 2017 by **Francis J. Shaw**

All rights reserved. No part of this publication may be reproduced, distributed or transmitted in any form or by any means, without prior written permission.

www.francisjshaw.com

Book Layout © 2017 BookDesignTemplates.com
Book Cover: kitfosterdesign.com

Breadcrumbs/ Francis J. Shaw. -- 1st ed.
Print Edition ISBN 978-1545003947

Dedication

For Julia
My beloved

"Beyond ideas of right and wrong, there is a field. I'll meet you there."

—Rumi

Contents

Introduction vii
Breadcrumbs 1
The King's Gambit 9
Crisis in Middle Earth 23
Progress and Timothy the Tortoise 37
The Sandman 77
The Butterfly Effect 85
The Special Theory of Spiritual Relativity 95
About the Author 113
Endnotes 115

Introduction

It is likely that from the moment language formed our ancestors sat around a campfire and told their first stories. They listened, they dreamed—long before writing, they remembered...for generations. Tales, yarns, legends and fables fill our human history, and stories are as powerful today as they have always been, but why?

Although we are more alike than different, we are also unique and our longing for answers to why each of us is here, is at the heart of storytelling—in our reading we are trying to find something hidden—the something that makes all the difference in our lives.

In this collection you will meet some familiar friends and perhaps make some new ones. In *Breadcrumbs*, we are on the yellow brick with Dorothy in the Wizard of Oz and in the woods with Hänsel and Gretel. Two seemingly very different stories, but could there be a key that unlocks both? *The King's Gambit* takes us on a very different journey—into the complex world of chess. All kinds of characters appear, and one makes a fateful decision that may have changed history. Next, we are with Frodo and the Fellowship of the Ring. Sitting on the mountaintop, staring at Mt. Doom, there's a *Crisis in Middle Earth* and it's not only the one you imagine. After arduous adventures with the hobbits, it's time a slow it down. Join me and Timothy the Tortoise, as we travel through time to answer a question—are we humans truly making progress? Next, picture this— you have been found guilty of a crime. Your execution is only moments away and your one hope is a wandering preacher your executioners dislike immensely. Just what was *The Sandman* doing? If you feel your story has come to a grinding halt, read *The Butterfly Effect*, as it's all about you, the most important room where you live, and what you may need to do to get your story moving forward if you are feeling stuck. Finally, join me and genius, Albert Einstein. I promise no theoretical physics skills are needed, because what I went seeking was a *Special Theory of Spiritual Relativity*. Did I find it?

Ready for some adventures? There's no need to pack. All you need is what every story asks of us—to be open to all the possibilities. I hope you find some nourishment to give you the strength to engage in the most important journey of discovery and mystery you can undertake—into your own depths, because stories summon us to pay attention to our own lives.

One

Breadcrumbs

Standing in a field of lavender, strolling on rolling hills, or resting by a brook as its waters gently meander through emerald green meadows, there is something strangely familiar about this place. Surrounded by beauty, with nothing to fear except what we make up; we draw a deep breath and begin the quest with a lingering question—what are we here to accomplish?

Dorothy's journey in the Wizard of Oz, started with a bang. Separated from the world she understood, her arrival caused the demise of the Wicked Witch of the East and further good fortune produced the kind, Good Witch of the North, with her magic white hat. Getting home should have been easy, but instead of being whisked away to Kansas;

she receives a kiss from the Good Witch for protection and directions on a road to take. To seek a wizard, who may or may not be able to help her, she is sent on her way with a pair of silver shoes. Hardly the most appropriate footwear for an adventure in a foreign land.

In another tale, Hänsel and Gretel had seen better times. Life, tough, and unforgiving is about to get a lot worse. With food scarce, they overhear a plan to abandon them deep in the forest, but Hänsel has a plan. Leaving a trail of stones, they can find their way back. Returning home doesn't produce the happy ending Hänsel hoped for, and the next time they are delivered even deeper into the woods to be left alone. Hänsel hatches another plan. Taking a loaf of bread, he leaves a trail of crumbs they can follow home. Their troubles intensify when birds eat the crumbs and the path is lost. A beautiful snow-white bird appears, showing them a trail to follow.

And our story? Our journey doesn't begin like Dorothy's. We don't arrive as heroes; our first shoes are more practical than magical and if there is a road for us to follow, it's poorly signposted and seldom golden. Like Hänsel, we build many plans and when they fail, we feel lost in our woods. Attempts to find our way, thwarted—feeling abandoned in places where the light struggles to penetrate—uncertain who to trust and what direction to pick—what nourishment to choose and what risks to take. Hating to make mistakes, we fear the unknown and when night comes and darkness descends, we cannot rest, because we are afraid. Unsure what to do, we make our journey about something else—bad luck, because some have it better; blaming others, because when something goes wrong it has to be someone's fault; unfair outcomes, because we feel we deserve happiness. Leaving our bread crumbs rotting in the soil, we fill our bags with memories, guilt, and regrets, dragging them along all the roads we encounter, hoping we can use them to find our way.

Dorothy, Hänsel and Gretel wanted to get home, and so do we. If "there is no greater power on earth than an idea whose time has come,"[1] what if the idea to come here was ours? What if we chose this journey, and if we did, why can't we trust we would have chosen well?

"There is meaning in every journey that is unknown to the traveler."[2] Like Dorothy and Hänsel and Gretel, our journey only truly begins when we don't know the way. To find out what we are here to accomplish, not only requires our life becomes an adventure before it's finished, but that we don't judge a road by its color.

In The Wonderful Wizard of Oz, the dangerous parts of Oz are woods inhabited with trees who acted like people. In the Harry Potter stories, there is a

Forbidden Forest near Hogwarts, containing giant spiders and other creatures. So often, forests are described as enchanted; places to avoid. Better to go around than encounter the monsters, witches, and magic dwelling within, but in both stories: The Wizard of Oz and Hänsel and Gretel, a greater significance is hidden in the details. One, which in our own journey's we stop seeing when spend time judging the path we find ourselves taking.

The Good Witch of the North, with her magic white hat, who blesses Dorothy with a kiss of protection, magic shoes, and a road to follow, doesn't promise an easy journey. She doesn't prevent the Wicked Witch of the West trying to steal Dorothy's shoes, but the mark left by her kiss keeps Dorothy from harm by the winged monkeys and contributes to the wizard agreeing to see Dorothy.

 In Hänsel and Gretel, the beautiful snow-white bird doesn't lead them to safety, but to the edible house of an old lady with a stick who plans to eat them. Once Gretel takes care of the witch, it's a white duck that helps them cross the water to safety.

The color white contains an equal balance of all the colors of the spectrum, including what we associate with the positive and negative aspects of other colors. It's the spirit of the white dove that guides us throughout our journey. The purity, wholeness, and perfection of home. It's not by our side to keep us away from what we are here to experience, learn and accomplish, but to remind us of the spiritual bread crumbs which are guiding our way—down yellow brick roads and on winding trails in the forest.

Through the twists and turns of life, we face many dilemmas on which road to take when we encounter forks along the way. We place pressure on ourselves to make what we believe are the best decisions, and as we stumble along, worries creep in. Our energy becomes focused on what's around the next corner or hiding in the shadows. Our perceptions blinded by what we agree to fear, lead us away from the awareness of who we truly are, to a place of unknowing, with only one conclusion we are sure about—we're not in Kansas anymore.

It's tempting to feel we made a mistake. Took a wrong turn or were led along the wrong trail. When something goes wrong we struggle to make sense of our experiences, and feel the need to apportion blame, most often to ourselves, to find solace. It's easy to be miserable and find others on the path, like the lion, tin man and scarecrow who understand, because they chose to believe the same story. The solution isn't found by seeking or fearing a wizard or a witch, but by simply reclaiming one important memory—we are here on a spiritual journey.

Once we acknowledge that truth, there is no need to focus on the destination because we already know there is no place like home, because we have been there. The key to our journeys is to recognize what we have, before we seek what we think we need. The silver shoes Dorothy wore could take her anywhere she wanted to go and she had them on since the beginning of her journey. The lion, who wanted courage, the tin man, a heart, and the scarecrow, a brain, all came to realize that they already had what they sought, and so do we.

The choice to embrace the gifts we came with changes how we approach our journey. Faith reveals there is nothing to fear behind the curtain or in the forest. The awareness that choices are not hurdles, but necessary steps for us to grow in our understanding of what we need to learn. Hope reminds us, although the road may be unfamiliar, the surroundings are not. In the majesty of towering trees and bright butterflies feeding on beautiful blooms, there are the familiar gifts of home that protect us from harm and surround us with love.

There is no need to fear on our spiritual journey for there are many roads, but it's all one path; where we are held, supported and loved all the way. Just like so many fairy tales, the hero must enter the forest and so must we. Danger is the lesson we need to teach us trust. Perhaps, resting at a crossroads in a clearing, we will remember the heavenly kisses of protection we received before we came and those lovingly imparted by our earthly mother to carry us forward. Feeling the bright white light within, come to realize what we are here to accomplish—to trust we are already half way home and clicking our heels twice, consider—that through the forest and over the rainbow is not that far to travel after all.

TWO

The King's Gambit

In 1999, Garik Weinstein fought a battle against overwhelming odds. One man versus 50,000 people in 75 countries and he triumphed. Fittingly, his first name, a variant of the name *Garrick*, meaning *spear* and *ruler*, banished the opposition over a four-month period. No one died in the conflict—at least no deaths were reported and although some egos may have been bruised, the victory was hard fought. Garik successfully ruled his kingdom for 15 years and most of his setbacks stemmed not from the tenacity of human foes, but from the mysterious domain of binary code. The 1999 contest introduced a new complexity into a game already full of huge variables, making it perhaps, the greatest game ever played.

Importance is best viewed with hindsight, as another game launched in 1999. Led by a Jordanian, Abu Musab al-Zarqawi, and adopting the black standard battle flag of Muhammad, the board is still in play. The roots of conflict are seldom as black and white as chess pieces; the goals cloaked behind rhetoric, deception, and misdirection. Interwoven in the match of 1999 and current events, is a story of a chosen people, the role of a king and rule of a kingdom. It begins, not with the nobility of achieving personal change through choice and endeavor, but with a catalyst that impacts the world we inherit from our ancestors—Garik was no exception.

He was born in Baku, Azerbaijan, to a Jewish father, whom he lost while still a child, and an Armenian mother. Prejudice is a burden many carry, driven by the roots of ancestors we have no control over. The child, Garik, faced uncertain prospects in chess, even if his light shone bright, because of a name and settled notions of heritage. The millions who left Europe for the shores of America confronted a similar problem—the desire to fit in. To be part of a new world, without baggage of past associations, whether they be race or creed, made for changes their great-grandchildren may be unaware of, even today. As the Irish, Italians, and Scandinavians desired to be seen first as Americans, so Garik sought a Russian identity. Adopting his mother's maiden name, *Gasparian*, aged twelve, and modifying it into Russian, he became Garry Kasparov.

In 2007, having retired from chess and embarked on a political career seeking democratic change, he reflected on his early years. In a 2007 Interview with David Remnick from the New Yorker, he said, "When you have to fight every day from a young age, your soul can be contradicted. I never really had it. Today, I have to be careful not to become cruel, because I became a soldier too early." There is sadness in these words. It's the same horror encountered at the sight of young children forced to join groups such as al-Zarqawi's, ISIL. The loss of formative years to follow a mortal king can destroy a piece of the future and limit many, sadly, to the life of a pawn. That Kasparov rose above the storm and conquered is an achievement to be recognized. There is much at stake in a battle for a king or a kingdom and religious faith is at the heart of the journey that connects chess, seekers of conquest through perceived divine guidance, and a covenant people.

It's said, a good story has a beginning, middle, and end. Chess also has three stages—opening, middlegame, and endgame. The most popular theory places its roots in Eastern India, but the earliest evidence is located in Persia, where it became part of educating the nobility. If India birthed the concept, it was the Muslim conquest of Persia that solidified the game. It came of age under their guidance. They developed the rules and it enabled a means to test military tactics without violence. They also provided the origin of terms we use in English. Both *check* and *chess* have their roots in the Persian word, *Shāh,* meaning *King.*

As the Muslim empire expanded, the game traveled along. Filtered on trade routes, one of its first stops was Russia. A perfect companion on long, cold, winter nights, its early exposure may be one reason for the dominance enjoyed by the people from the *Land of Rus.* Spreading into Europe, largely through Moorish Spain, Christians embraced the game. No doubt they saw the same benefits as Muslims and inevitably when cultures and spiritual worlds collide, there are casualties and change.

Before the bishop of Christendom appeared on the board, the role was held by the elephant. In Buddhism, a symbol of mental strength, where the gray elephant symbolized an uncontrolled mind and the white, a tamed mind. As the battle for souls and territory continued, the white bishop of Rome as head of the Holy Roman Empire was seldom tame.

The piece beside the king, originally an adviser or *Vizier,* with limited moves, became the Queen, with powers to leap across the board. The change may have reflected medieval Europe, where the role of women had evolved. When powerful queens were not ruling in their own right, they were often a strong presence behind the reign of the king, or as daughters, married into the houses of nobility to build alliances. Despite these apparent gains, the game can continue without a Queen, but not the king, as King Henry VIII of England demonstrated on several occasions.

In 1209 the white bishop, Pope Innocent III, ordered a crusade to destroy the Cathar heresy. Within the stronghold of Béziers a mixture of Cathars and good Catholics sought shelter. Walls breached, how would they know who to kill? Arnaud Amalric, the Papal legate, allegedly uttered, '*Caedite eos. Novit enim Dominus qui sunt eius.*' - 'Kill them all, God will know his own.'

Although conflicts between Christians and Muslims continued, the battle for the heavenly King turned inward. Eliminating the Cathars and the Knights Templar signaled a new struggle. When Martin Luther played a bold move and pinned his 95 theses to All Saints' Church in Wittenberg, igniting the Reformation, the Christians separated into Protestants and Catholics. The king castled—a bystander, as the people of one faith pit rook against bishop; knights charging...pawns dying. Perhaps, God no longer recognized his own.

By the age of enlightenment, the battle on the board shifted to empire building and introspective thinkers focused on invention and self-improvement. Benjamin Franklin said, "The Game of chess is not merely an idle amusement; several very valuable qualities of the mind, useful in the course of human life, are to be acquired and strengthened by it, so as to become habits ready on all occasions; for life is a kind of chess, in which we have often points to gain, and competitors or adversaries to contend with, and in which there is a vast variety of good and ill events, that are, in some degree, the effect of prudence, or the want of it. By playing at chess then, we may learn foresight, circumspection, and caution."[3]

As the 20th century launched, Franklin's dream of prudence became a nightmare of terror, as the world embroiled in bitterness, lost its sense. For the Jews, persecution was the shadow relentlessly following their every move. A people, chosen by God, without a homeland, hounded by an old hate that hindered every hope of finding acceptance. When the Nazi's told Jews they had to wear a yellow badge to identify themselves, their ancestors must have cried out in anguish. Whatever disagreements leaders and countries had with each other, they always made space to create time to persecute everybody's common enemy and historical scapegoat.

In Europe, 1090, light and dark squares were introduced to the chess board. The crusades raged— to the Christians there were those of the true faith and dark ones, separated from the heavenly light. In 1215, Pope Innocent III declared, "Jews and Saracens (the generic term used for Muslims in the medieval era) of both sexes in every Christian province and at all times shall be marked off in the eyes of the public from other peoples through the character of their dress."[4] Others joined to shame those whose beliefs would challenge the king.

In 1269, King Louis IX of France, later a catholic saint, decreed that French Jews must wear a round yellow badge on their breast and back. Followed in 1274, by Edward I of England, who enacted the Statute of Jewry, which denoted, each Jew, after seven years of age, should wear a distinguishing mark on an outer garment in the form of two tables joined, of yellow felt of the length of six inches and of the breadth of three inches. Neither the swastika nor the yellow patches are original inventions of the Nazi's—nor is the hate and prejudice. They are blunt forces that only require a pointing figure, a way to identify the targets, willing warriors, and a propaganda machine to sell the message.

With hindsight, removing tyrants and dictators appears to be an earnest strategy, which democracies continue to advocate and enforce when it suits, but behind the rhetoric is a lesson still unlearned. Between 1618 and 1648, Europe entered a brutal conflict. Initially pitting Protestant states against catholic rivals, the conflict widened. The cause? Who would fill the void as the Holy Roman Empire crumbled. The removal of figures like Saddam

Hussein, Gaddafi, and destabilization in Syria, Afghanistan, and Egypt, created another void for groups like ISIL. Like 17th century Christians, the conflict began by killing members of their own faith before spreading to other less desirable's. Is their real aim to create an Islamic State led by religious authority or is it the same smokescreen employed by European countries during the Thirty Years war? An agenda, more about power and founding a mortal kingdom, than whose definition of a heavenly King should rule. ISIL has threatened another Holocaust against the Jews, vowing to raise their black flag in Jerusalem. Perhaps in their desire to create a Caliphate, they have forgotten many Caliphs from long ago were expert chess players, and to become masters of the board is not found by destruction or even winning—not in the sense we believe.

According to a survey by the World Chess Federation (FIDE), 600 million play chess regularly—more than followers of Buddhism, Sikhism, and Judaism, combined. Players are not seeking a religious experience, so what is the draw? (No pun intended)—Reasoning, planning, analysis, creativity, and critical thinking, all form part of the chess experience. A Chinese proverb says, *"Life is like a game of chess, changing with each move,"* and life and chess share problem solving as the beating heart that drives both games. But, what is the problem we need to solve? For chess players and seekers of life's purpose or a heavenly kingdom, one eye is always on the most important piece—the king.

Chess is about the ability to recognize patterns and imagine all the possibilities. A battle of minds, not armies, it requires an understanding where survival hinges on sacrifice as much as boldness, so where do we find such skills?

Gary Kasparov's father was an electrical engineer and both parents of the current world champion, Magnus Carlsen, are also engineers. Jews have been playing chess since the 12th century and of the first thirteen undisputed world champions over 50% were Jewish. Judit Polgár, the youngest Grandmaster in history (male or female), of Hungarian Jewish roots, is the strongest woman player of all time, holding the number one ranking for women players for 26 years. When Kasparov was asked about his religion in a 2007 Fox News interview with James Rosen, he replied, "I would call myself a Christian. Sort of self-appointed, but I am indifferent to that." It doesn't matter. Something in the history and genes of the Jewish people makes them expert chess players—so what could it be?

Of 22,000 games played between 1999 and 2002 by players with a FIDE Elo rating above 2,500 (Senior Master and Grandmaster), the most common result was a draw, with 55% ending in that outcome.[5]

Governments relish victory and to utter '*mission accomplished,*' a reflection of correct policy and why the electorate made the right choice. But, of the games won, relatively few end with checkmate. On most occasions resignation occurs first. To capitulate is not always the end game, as it signifies the end of a battle, not necessarily the war. To understand chess we have to embrace survival, and none have faced more determined attempts at annihilation than the Jewish people.

As wanderers, so long without a homeland they have endured. Settlements always at risk and with no standing army, they repeatedly searched for a place beyond the long arm of persecution. Surviving the terrible onslaught of the Holocaust, Israel's position remains isolated, surrounded by more enemies than friends. Perhaps they understand that winning in the chess of life is not about enforcing doctrine, conquering, nor destruction, but resigning to keeping faith with your king—no matter what.

Raised in the catholic minority of England, I might have a better feeling of the terrible obstacles Jewish people have faced if I had lived at another time. I may have become indifferent to some catholic teaching, but I am drawn to Mary as the Queen of Heaven (there is something very comforting about having a heavenly mother to stand by my king) and the saints, like the prophets of ancient times. Having extra help from those who have overcome is a comfort. St. Teresa of Avila (1515-1582), the patron saint of chess players, wrote, "I hope you do not think I have written too much about this already; for I have only been placing the board, as they say. You have asked me to tell you about the first steps in prayer; although God did not lead me by them, my daughters I know no others, and even now I can hardly have acquired these elementary virtues. But you may be sure that anyone who cannot set out the pieces in a game of chess will never be able to play well, and, if he does not know how to give check, he will not be able to bring about a checkmate. Now you will reprove me for talking about games, as we do not play them in this house and are forbidden to do so. That will show you what kind of a mother God has given you -- she even knows about vanities like this! However, they say that the game is sometimes legitimate. How legitimate it will be for us to play it in this way, and, if we play it frequently, how quickly we shall give checkmate to this Divine King! He will not be able to move out of our check nor will He desire to do so."[6]

History can be a great teacher. It even repeats in some form, and yet, why are we such poor students? It's *"The $64 question,"* a popular 1940's American catchphrase, used for any difficult question or problem (it later morphed into the *$64,000 Question* game show in 1955). Coincidently or not, 64 is the number of squares on a chess board and as we each struggle to understand opponents thinking, the current game is once again setting a problem to solve. Creating instability provides a clear choice—do we kill and destroy for the mortal kingdom or trust and have faith in the heavenly King, so once again he can recognize his own.

When Innocent III and Martin Luther were not pursuing religious change, they played chess. It's unknown how the game influenced their decision-making, for better or worse, and it's not playing the game, but what we learn in the playing that matters the most. As I study the board, I am imagining the possibilities...praying for all sides that we don't become cruel, but find the foresight to see that we all born of an engineer creator—who asks us to build in the spaces we move to.

My hand is on my king and my head is pounding. Once I release, I know there is no going back. I contemplate a prayer to St. Teresa, who is the patron saint of headaches as well as chess, when I remember a man who had a vision about a stairway to heaven. His name is Jacob (Yaqub in Arabic) and he is a patriarch of Islam and the Israelites. The dream occurred when he left the town of Beersheba, home to the most chess grandmasters per capita in the world. Perhaps there, studying engineering at the Ben Gurion University, is a Father or Mother, who can pass on a message through a child, to all faiths and those with none at all, that Jacob's ladder is one we can all climb together without killing each other—an endgame that finishes with a draw for all.

We will never escape conflict and no matter how hard we work to find peaceful solutions, there are times when those who persecute, terrorize, and torture non-combatants will not listen. Our lives are a gift and in difficult circumstances we face a choice— either fight to defend our right to be here, or be willing to give up our lives non-violently. Perhaps that is why chess is so important, because by playing, we open ourselves to the possibility of finding peaceful outcomes.

"When he had not yet decided to devote himself to politics, and, as a twenty-year old without any plans for the future, was a drifter in Vienna, he frequented the chess cafes of that city, sitting there for entire nights. The game fascinated him so much that he feared it could, as it had so many others, totally absorb him, and take over his life. Therefore, he decided to break with it overnight."[7] The man's name was Adolf Hitler.

THREE

Crisis in Middle Earth

After an arduous adventure, the journey was finally over. With the ring destroyed in Mount Doom, we rejoiced, the evil banished to the depths could never rise again. Along the way, we encountered a wise wizard; mystical elves, a dashing king; enough champions to cheer on, and they were just the supporting cast. For Tolkien, gave us Frodo and his hobbit friends—the very small ground dwellers with large feet and even bigger appetites. They were the real heroes he chose.

We love an underdog. Being small and a hero in any world, real or imagined, is no easy matter, but such bravery seemed beyond my comprehension. I would need to look elsewhere to find myself in the story. The swashbuckling Aragorn appealed, apart from his constant unwashed hair, as did the magic tricks of Gandalf and the pluck of Gimli the dwarf, but to imagine myself, as one of them would be an even greater stretch. I was out of characters...except for one...Sméagol: the nasty bulgy eyed creature, for whom an average day consisted of eating raw fish, scheming, and talking to a sparkling gold ring in a dark cave. It wasn't a pleasant thought, but like Sméagol, the middle-aged man with little hair I see when I look into the mirror, was also once someone else.

We begin this journey the same, naked in body and memories of where we have come from. Although our entry here is quite dramatic, the first age of our lives begins with only observation. We look and listen for quite some time before we utter anything other than cries and gibberish. Child development experts may have good explanations on why it has to be this way, but I wonder if non-human reasons are also part of why we start our journey here in the quietness, experiencing a peace we may spend the rest of our lives trying to rediscover.

Although we rely on others to provide for our needs, there is something quite rebellious in our nature. Our silent beginnings and our early words built around physical and mental chewing, as we examine the world in conversations centered on the 'what' of our surroundings. When we do encounter the first questions where we can provide a response, our answers are more often in the negative—replying with 'no' more than 'yes.' It's true that we don't like being told what to do and part of being here is the need to make up our own minds, but is it also something deeper? In some studies, young children have shared their recollections of where they were before coming here. With many similar story elements and the doubtful conclusion that it's all made up, perhaps our first desire to disagree is no more than a memory that the answers our earthly guardians provide are often wrong, and we know it.

By around five years of age, our memories of home have faded. Forced to accept our new environment without prior knowledge soothing the bumps on our path, our questions also change, from 'what' to 'why.' In the beginning were the words and the words were confusing, but our new abilities with language now demand explanations to our observations. For parents, having just survived the *terrible twos*, the constant questioning requires a new strength and it can't be a coincidence that right at this moment, when we express a burning desire to seek understanding, we are dispatched to school for compulsory education. It almost feels like a punishment.

Apart from creating space for parents, the timing appears logical—*we* have questions. With a whole team of teachers, qualified in different areas and disciplines awaiting our arrival, it appears like a match in heaven, but is it? The education world we now inhabit is firmly behind imparting information and knowledge, caring more about adherence and compliance and little for answering our many questions. Yanked away from the freedom of play, embraced out of desire, hunger, and joy, we experience the first of many diversions from the path, just as our feet feel planted. Although we don't remember, it is perhaps our first experience of loss. A theme we will struggle to understand, for most, if not all, of our lives.

It's also the beginning of another transformation, away from the freedom to imagine and create, to rigidity, conformity, and rules. It seems logical. We need to know the rules so we know when we break them, but other changes are more subtle. The letters we learned, to form the words, to communicate our feelings, ideas, and dreams…have new rivals. Behind every moment of our lives is the mathematics of structure and equations to keep us focused and goal-oriented along the road to success as others define it, and paths to reach it. Routine, sold as our Savior, to be our guiding light and capture us in the spell of repetition. Each day the alarm bell rings to usher in the 60 minutes of each hour, 24 hours of each day, and 365 days of each year. We count everything that matters and when we celebrate the unique event of our own birth, it is around a number—the kick-off to a ticking clock which will someday stop.

We agree to the plan because we have to and any sense of our own mortality is somewhere on a far off land we have no desire to visit. Just as we see the light at the end of our school-days tunnel, we rebel. Not since our early days has such passion reached the surface. We question everything and although society may excuse this brief interlude as a rite of passage into adulthood, perhaps its purpose is the first wake-up call to break free of the chains of conformity. A nudge to chase our purpose beyond the bounds of the framework drilled into our being for the past many years of education.

As the first age ends and the second begins, we are full of information. Our teachers hope it's knowledge and we are thoroughly prepared for the next stage of our lives, but are we? All those school years provided a regimen we endured and learned to navigate and although we saw glimpses of the adult world, once we arrive, it feels foreign. History, taught what happened to others; mathematics, angels, equations, multiplication; geography, the names of countries and capitals...but for many, there was no life map, no quest, no *Fellowship of the Ring*, no greater purpose to grab and call their own.

Transitioning into adulthood can leave us with a sense of confusion. We want to be confident, secure in knowing what to do and how, because after years of education we feel we are supposed to know.

Unfortunately, what school didn't teach are other necessary skills that touch every facet of our journey for the rest of our lives—how to build healthy relationships with others and ourselves. Adulthood doesn't provide classrooms, a teacher and text books to digest. It's why we have so many awkward moments and easily fall into patterns where blame and avoidance become the go to feelings and actions.

The second age lasts anywhere from twenty to thirty years and lays the foundation for our lives. We go searching for purpose and meaning. To establish ourselves in work and relationships and to pursue goals we hope will lead to success and contentment. They are the years we have the most questions—who will we meet to share our life...where are we heading...how will we get there...when will we find happiness?

We experience responsibility and accountability, success and failure, joy and rejection. We spend much time and energy on our 'wants,' and despite our best efforts, lessons keep returning until we learn what we need to grow. Change is a constant companion we love or hate, depending on what it brings us and then when we are around halfway home we experience disappointment, anxiety, and a drop in self-confidence. Although these have been our companions before, there is an increase in their intensity and combined with fragile emotions, melancholy and sorrows rise to the surface.

If there is a watchword that sums up our heightened brain activity and amplified worries, it's *confusion*. Although we may be aware of transformation in our bodies—hair loss or graying, changes in weight, and having less energy before we feel tired, there are other factors at play. For men, who often judge their self-worth by work accomplishments it's often a time to reassess career goals and whether the results match the vision they had long ago. For some, Thomas Merton's words provide a painful truth and little consolation—"People may spend their whole lives climbing the ladder of success only to find, once they reach the top, the ladder is leaning against the wrong wall."

Women are also experiencing changes and not just hormone adjustments. For much of their lives they have fulfilled multiple roles, which may have included a combination of motherhood, a career, and frequently responsibility for caring for family members—there is often a strong desire to create a different future. As the earthquake of these events shake up the lives of men and women, the loss of important relationships, like parents, adds to the growing list of pressures. As though it's a last chance, we are pulled to anything that makes us feel young again, perhaps in the hope that we can return to who we once were. In 1965, psychologist Elliot Jaques gave us two words to surmise his findings...midlife crisis—the third age of our lives.

Back in Middle Earth, Frodo experienced his own changes. The great quest wasn't going well. The *Fellowship of the Ring* starting with such hope was in disarray. Gandalf, his larger than life wizard, believed lost to a very upset dragon and the others scattered to who knows where. Perched on a rocky hilltop, tired and worn out by the burden he carried, he looked toward Mount Doom and realized the awful truth of his journey—despite all his adventures and losses, there was no going back.

Every story has a beginning, middle, and end. Each has a protagonist faced with a question and a problem they need to solve. It's why the most important part of any story is the middle, because halfway through every story something profound and impactful presents itself. It's where Frodo found himself, thinking of home and perhaps wondering why it wasn't the biggest, the strongest, or the wisest, called to undertake such a hard journey.

Reaching the mid-peak of our lives, with more years behind than those left ahead, we have spent much of our time asking the who, what, when, where, why, and how questions. We may be satisfied with some answers we have found, while others sit in limbo waiting to rise to the surface again, but what we need now is not an old question, but a new one, because our midlife *is* a crisis. There is more to it than we imagine because no matter what has occurred in our lives: successes and failures, we have been comfortable far too long. We are dying and our future is dependent on how we react to what we experience as we sit confused on our mountaintop. Our response to the discomfort we feel.

What we learn and experience in life only gets us halfway down the path. The rest comes from within and the reminders begin in midlife. We are meant to get lost because it's the only way we can hear the voice calling out to us to connect with ourselves in our own story. Sméagol lost himself in his—he chased after the wrong 'precious.' It's the reason why we are captivated by crime novels. There is a mystery to uncover in our lives and the first step is to recognize the confusion we experience in midlife is not an invitation to judge our memories or attempt to go back to the past through youthful actions. The new zest for life we feel is the burst of energy we need, not to relive the journey we have had, but to accomplish what is left to do—to begin the last adventure and find the key to unlock the mystery of our lives.

Although much of life revolves around work it's not our purpose for being here, no matter what it brings. If you have journeyed with someone dying the words they speak are never, 'I wished I worked more.' As we move closer to that time for each of us, we need to re-examine the clues, because midlife is not about confusion, but a calling to find our individual purpose for being here. It's no coincidence that we worry less about what people think of us as we age, because it just gets in the way. It's no coincidence that we daydream less as we grow older, because the time for chasing shadows is over.

Frodo could have stayed content in the Shire, as can we, in ours. We can choose to manage the changes we experience as best we can or embrace the courage to seek the mystery. Choosing the second option is no easy path. Before Frodo said he would carry the ring, all he heard were reasons from others why it couldn't be done and how many of those present wouldn't work with some of the others even to try. Something in Frodo made him say yes and if we are going to respond to our call, it's going to take asking one last question—a power question, unlike those we posed before.

It's not a simple matter, to be taking lightly, because what we decide to ask is going to shape the journey to come and we can never look at life the same way again. We may not fully understand the change or impact, but like Frodo, there is no going back. It changes us, differently, as though we have been awoken from a dream, and the view of consequences we once had also changes, because time is running out. We realize we are standing on the arc of the rainbow we have sought and our quest for meaning changes.

For years, we developed complex coping mechanisms but haven't found resolution. Midlife brings together all the feelings and turmoil to the surface with a clear message—we are meant to get to this point in our lives. We spend so much time dragging around our history. It contains our regrets, perceived errors and judgments and although it may be tempting to make confusion the culprit, what the middle of our story is really offering is clarity. It's the letting go of what we thought we knew and understood that is the real turmoil.

We have focused so much of lives on an outward looking journey, when we are suddenly presented with a new life altering fact—the real journey...the real purpose for our lives is an inward journey. We shouldn't be surprised. We didn't arrive with jobs, clothes, houses, or cars and life is not about attaining them. We came with other gifts inside and despite trying to push them aside as myth; we need a powerful nudge to take them seriously, but we have worked hard to build our vision and it won't die easy. Our first reaction is to rebel, because we struggle to see that all we have achieved so far doesn't have the value we have assigned to it. Our illusions are shattered and buying the sports car or having plastic surgery is just stubborn resistance to hold on to a past that won't deliver a future.

I find myself in the midpoint of my life and I am letting my power question drive me forward—*what am I supposed to learn*? It fills me, not with dread, but with a hunger to find my place in my story. I see, that I have at times been all the characters in Tolkien's tale—moments when I have been a wizard, a hero, a stubborn dwarf, and an adventurous hobbit. Even, when I was lost, unkind, or inconsiderate, seeing Sméagol when I gaze in the mirror, I knew that he was once Gollum, a hobbit, and could be again.

And Frodo? If you have watched the wonderful Lord of the Rings trilogy by Peter Jackson, you may also want to read Tolkien's books, because it's there you read that Frodo Baggins was 50 years old when the Fellowship of the Ring was formed—middle age called out to him to begin a new adventure. There is much to admire in Frodo's journey, as there is when we look at our own. We just might see the difference we make when we risk all. We can make excuses; stay confused. We can read Frodo's story and dismiss it as unrealistic fiction. We can dismiss our own as the same. We can decide, the small folk in this world cannot challenge the powerful who seek the ring, but for me, it's not the most important part of Frodo's story. It's the knowledge he had. Even if he could safely cross Middle Earth, without being killed and destroy the ring under the nose of such great evil, there was no going back to the life he had in the Shire. His path, like ours, is not to return somewhere we have been, but to end up somewhere we have not. Aptly, Tolkien sent Frodo to the 'Undying Lands,' and the thought of it being there for all of us, is enough to embrace midlife as an opportunity and not a burden of confusion.

Tolkien's fourth age begins with the destruction of the ring and the ascent of man and I am looking forward to what mine will bring, because the past has had its time with me. An adventure still beckons me forward, into the mystery, because the journey has always been clear—life is the 'precious' to seek.

FOUR

Progress and Timothy the Tortoise

Today, we have plenty of options to connect with each other. If we want to see and hear our leaders, we can do so from the comfort of home, wrapped up snugly in front of a scrolling electric world that feeds our yearning for information and stimulus. 700 years ago, our forbearers new little of those who governed their lives and most seldom traveled more than ten miles away from their birthplace their entire lives. In 16th century England, mostly during the summer months, the monarch traveled around the realm meeting their subjects, having a wonderful time; eating, hunting, and reminding people who was the boss. Those chosen to host the large entourage, both excited and stressed, as entertaining the king or queen was an expensive and challenging honor. These journeys were called a *Royal Progress.*

Progress from the Latin, *Progressus,* translates as 'an advance or going forward,' and visiting the 20th century to the present; to the strides made in science, medicine, and technology, it's tempting to say we have never progressed so fast or so well. Or, is it possible there are other times in our history that we would have felt the same way?

The 18th century introduced new vigor to the ideals of progress and the goals of the Enlightenment movement. Liberty, progress, reason, and tolerance, were some of the goals they espoused. Fresh on the heels of the luminaries who imparted new philosophies were the scientists and inventors marveling the world with machines and contraptions, which would make business more productive and our lives full of wonder.

In May, 1851, the Great Exhibition opened in London, providing a venue for showing off the fruits of the industrial revolution, economic gains, and increased per capita growth. It was an incredible spectacle. As 6 million visitors marveled at the exhibits over the course of 5 months, it's doubtful too many were grown up children from the early 1800's at the dawn of the industrial revolution. Any that had survived the long hours and terrible working conditions now had children of their own and probably had conversations we would instantly recognize.

Looking haggard, the twelve year old slumps onto a kitchen stool. "How was work, son?" his mother asks.

"Long..." he murmurs.

"It was a lot harder when I was your age. Oh yes...let me tell you..."

No, please don't...he wanted to say, but he was too tired to bother.

She was right. Progress, slow and painful, had arrived from the days of the 'dark, satanic mills,'[8] In Britain, the 1847 Ten Hour Act, cut the hours for women and those under eighteen to ten hours a day. An improvement to the previous twelve hours a day, Monday through Friday, and nine hours on Saturdays. However, history is seldom a consolation, especially to the young. If he were to live another 40 years, exceeding the average life expectancy for the time, he would have witnessed the founding of the Society for the Prevention of Cruelty to Children, in 1891. A full 67 years after the founding of the Society for the Prevention of Cruelty to Animals, in 1824.

Bouncing his grandson on his knee, he might ponder, the shortest distance between two points may be a straight line, but the path of *progress*, follows a more mysterious trail.

The year 1855 seemed like many others around the same time and considering how much conflict simultaneously occurs in the world, it was a quiet year, except for the Crimean War, beginning in 1853. As Timothy the tortoise, ships mascot aboard HMS Queen, set off to war, he, like many others, may have been confused over the reasons for the impending conflict. Seemingly over control of religious sites in the Holy Land, this was not a religious conflict, nor a tyrant removal operation. Rather, Russia saw the possibilities of extending their influence as the Ottoman Empire headed into decline. While England and France, fearing a negative impact to their interests in the region, sided with the Turks against the Russian 'Bear.'

Owning Empires was a messy business and as one of 33 conflicts Britain fought during the 19th century, the Crimean War, like so many, didn't contain much of taking the moral high ground. What it did have in buckets were incompetent leaders on all sides, who unknowingly conspired to mess up at every opportunity. As public opinion grew against the conflict, it thankfully ended in 1856, along (in 1855) with the British government which launched the whole mess.

Perhaps fittingly, in 1856, Queen Victoria inaugurated the Victoria Cross, for valor. The common soldier had suffered much and they deserved another type of

Royal Progress. There was also something for the 19th century science nerds. The war had showcased some technology firsts—the role of the telegraph, use of the railways, and one of the first conflicts recorded using the relatively new media of photography. Still, one can only ponder that as the last shots were fired, the words on people's lips were Poet Laureate, Alfred Tennyson's, in his catchy take on the futile Charge of the Light Brigade into the 'valley of death in 1854.'

> 'Theirs not to make reply,
> Theirs not to reason why,
> Theirs but to do and die.[9]

Despite three fires, HMS Queen and Timothy the tortoise survived the war. No doubt glad to leave his sea legs behind and feel 'England's green and pleasant land'[10] under his feet once again.

Perhaps we would like to think of progress as linear events that gently arc, as it's a picture that provides comfort of being on the right path. If events of the 1850's have any wisdom to share, we would expect to see it, brightly shinning as the midday sun. For in 1855, the word *progress* was mentioned more times in English writing, than any previous year or in any year since.[11]

We would expect to see an increase in the usage of words like *progress* during the final moments of impactful world events (it peaks at both ends of the two world wars). Although Russia lost the most in the treaty that ended the Crimean conflict, Timothy the tortoise won as much as anyone else, by getting to go home. As the sun dipped beneath the Crimean horizon, perhaps the illumination of *progress* had a different light source.

It's winter, 1854, and as darkness fills the Crimean sky and the medical staff retire for the night, a tall, slender woman with brown hair covered by a white cap, makes her way around the wards for a last check. She believes in cleanliness, but not germs, and since arriving with her volunteers the death rate has increased. Her name is Florence Nightingale.

'She is a "ministering angel" without any exaggeration in these hospitals, and as her slender form glides quietly along each corridor, every poor fellow's face softens with gratitude at the sight of her. When all the medical officers have retired for the night and silence and darkness have settled down upon those miles of prostrate sick, she may be observed alone, with a little lamp in her hand, making her solitary rounds.'[12] It was this report in The Times that gave her the name all school children remember learning—'The Lady with the Lamp.'

In their later years, when the men who survived the winter of 1854 wrote their memoirs, they talked about the lantern carrier who wandered in the darkness. The love they felt just because she was there, not because she saved them. Their suffering eased by her presence and how they could kiss her shadow in gratitude as it fell before them. Florence revolutionized nursing; founding the world's first secular nursing school and International Nurses Day is celebrated on her birthday.

It had to be the answer. *Progress* isn't found under a burning sun that shines reason upon mankind, but through the soft glow of candlelight. There, in the shadows, truth revealed itself—poor leadership and a pointless war brought a realization, that we as a race would not move forward without holding compassion and healing close to our hearts. The song of the Nightingale that would banish the futility of war, forever...answer found...essay completed...

Pause...The light of the lamp wasn't the solution—Timothy returned to the high seas and within a few short years the worst kind of war erupted, when civil war broke out in the America's. Despite a great leader in Lincoln and correcting a great wrong by freeing the slaves, the use of *progress* in writing continued to decline.

Timothy retired from the navy in 1892. Welcomed by the Earl of Devon at Powderham Castle, he received the family motto, etched on his underside—"Where have I fallen? What have I done?" Questions humanity continued to ask as further conflicts ensued. During the Second World War, Timothy prepared, by moving from his favorite wisteria bed, to an air raid shelter he dug under the terrace steps.

Time passed, the hands of the doomsday clock progressing closer to the end. Further definitions added to *progress* provided more substance. We were no longer only 'moving forward,' but 'gradually improving' and 'developing in a positive way.' Despite this clarity of wishful thinking, in 1968 it changed again for the worse.

As the Vietnam War continued to rage, the North Vietnamese launched a surprised Tet offensive turning public opinion about the conflict. Martin Luther King and Robert Kennedy were assassinated and starvation gripped parts of Africa. Students launched mass demonstrations around the world and The Guardian newspaper in England called 1968, 'The year that changed history.'

When the dust settled, the steadiness of the usage of *progress* over the previous twenty years took a drastic turn downwards. The end of the Vietnam War and civil rights legislation did nothing to stem the tide. It seemed once again, that whatever light we encountered at the end of the tunnel was never enough to stop the dissatisfaction with the direction we were heading. A disturbing historical pattern kept repeating. Public opinion, often driven by the young, would swell against a perceived ethical wrong or unwise course of action, until it could no longer be ignored. The powerful would fight against change, kicking and screaming, as leaders and peacemakers emerged to combat senseless conflicts and correct moral codes. We had come so far and yet moved so little. Worse, it appeared that only certain types of progress would be allowed by the powerful and no leaders who espoused peaceful outcomes would be allowed to survive. "Is it progress if a cannibal uses a fork?"[13]

Driving down the street by where I live, two raised stone flower beds protrude from both sides of the pavement, narrowing the road so little space remains for two cars to pass. A speed bump lies between the flower beds and signs indicate a change in the road rules. One says that the previous speed limit (30km/h) is no longer in force and another bigger blue sign, contains pictures of a car, house, adult pedestrian, and a child kicking a ball. Once you cross the speed bump you have entered a *Traffic Calming* zone (literal translation of the German word, *Verkehrsberuhigung*).

The rules of our traffic calming zone state that cars may not exceed 7 km/h, pedestrians may use the entire street, and children are permitted to play in the road. There is one problem with our traffic calming zone. The cars seldom stay beneath 7 km/h because they don't need to. The pedestrians stick to the pavement and there are no children kicking a ball around in the street. Not today, nor I doubt tomorrow...not once have I seen a child playing there, in all the time I have lived here.

Despite opportunities and initiatives to slow down and reflect after years like 1968 and what followed, a different world emerged. In some ways it is a natural occurring progressive phenomenon, where each generation views the previous one with some disdain, mild amusement, or a look that says, 'what planet are you from?' So much has changed since the days of my childhood, I shouldn't be surprised that it seems so strange to the young of today, but I am.

My childhood was in a year BC (before computers) and it seems hard for a child of today to imagine a time like this ever existed. How impossible life must have been without a smart phone and a constant fast Internet connection. I could tell them we didn't even have electronic calculators and still used an abacus to do sums. I could show them a picture of what one looked like. Even though it may look like something a baby would play with, it was in fact a counting machine used for over 4,500 years. I could tell them how we played outside almost every day, no matter the weather. How many times I would not listen to my mother calling me to come in because I liked it so much. I could tell them how we loved to take rambles in the countryside using a compass and a map to navigate.

I could...but perhaps only Timothy, back enjoying retirement in his wisteria bed would understand these old ways. The world had changed. It wasn't overnight, but even today it feels like it happened very fast...fast because what the world did, was speed up. The technological revolution and industrial revolution both centered on delivering increased productivity. Mailing letters became obsolete as has talking to each other face to face to a large degree. Now, we have more options. We can email, text, and chat with anyone around the world in seconds, inventing new languages as we go and the virtual world has become the new playground of our children. It's progressive, but is it *progress?* Or is it as Aldous Huxley said, that, "technology progress has merely provided us with more efficient means for going backwards?"

Having more choices to communicate doesn't automatically make us better communicators, but one of the hallmarks of this technical age has been to sell us new things—not just products, but abilities. To cope with new expectations we would need some tools, upgrades, and a delivery system to connect everything together. We could forget about playing outside with friends or communing with neighbors; the whole world was at our fingertips—it needed us. Smart phones epitomized this new age. With a wealth of information on the Internet and apps for almost everything, we were running out of excuses why life wasn't better—why we were not happier.

Our brains also needed an upgrade to cope and without warning we had to become multitaskers. If multitasking didn't appear front and center on our resumes, our chances of landing a job in the new world could be in doubt. This surely was an example of *progress*. To acknowledge a skill we all had, but didn't know we did, until it was suddenly needed. Maybe I was sick the day they taught multitasking at school or was it just a ghost in the machine? Either way, it wasn't a problem—we all bought it. After all, it feels good to know to we can do many things so well; all at the same time. There was only one small problem—we can't.

Science also took huge leaps in the technological revolution. Scientists have conducted many experiments and MRI scans to determine what happens in the brain when we multi-task. It was bad news—our brains are built to process one thing at a time. When we multi-task it affects the brain's learning systems, and as a result, we do not learn as well when we are distracted. We also try to fool our brains with parallel processing. This is where we tell the brain to think about one item separate from another, but we tell the brain to focus on each one with the same importance. The brain does its best to cope, but seldom delivers because each time we switch tasks the brain has to start over, so everything takes longer. Result—we become less productive.

The news gets worse.

All memory is not created equal. E.g. for remembering how to ride a bicycle we use procedural memory, but for learning facts and concepts we use declarative memory. When multitasking, declarative memory is disrupted. It's not much help knowing you can still peddle your bike when your focus needs to be analyzing facts and figures for an important presentation. To muddy the waters a little more, the brain accesses the hippocampus, a critical area for recalling information. When we multi-task the brain closes it down and uses the striatum, which is geared to learning new skills and not recalling information.

Many will read this and still insist they are great multitaskers and no doubt more memory pills will continue to appear on the market to ease our remembering issues. If we didn't understand the full truth about something as small as multitasking, which might be hindering our progress, perhaps more impactful information is having a deeper impact.

Many countries favor using Gross Domestic Product (GDP) as a way to measure the economic health of a nation and an implied link to population well-being. Overall, we appear to be doing quite well with some nations growing every year. GDP measures the market value of all goods produced, but it's good to remember that the 'G' in GDP stands for gross. A calculation for net isn't included, which means it only measures what is produced and not the costs it takes to produce.

That doesn't sound quite so good. GDP also counts crime as a benefit as it includes costs for legal and medical fees and repairs to damaged property. Another inclusion with GDP is pollution. What it costs to create and what it takes to fix, are both included. Also, GDP does not count work that is done for free, like volunteering, or take into account the harm that some economic activity can do to an economy. GDP does not take into account the distribution of wealth in a country or the amount of leisure time people have.

When we are sick and go to the doctor we are often measured. Depending on our symptoms, this can include blood pressure, pulse, weight, heart rhythm etc. To fully diagnose what was occurring with *progress*, I would need to look beyond one measure. The Genuine Progress Indicator (GPI) assesses variables related to economic, social, and environmental progress. As GDP and the GPI are both measured in monetary terms, they can be compared on the same scale.

Unlike GDP, GPI counts all work; paid or unpaid as having value. It subtracts the cost of pollution and increases as the poor receive a greater portion of national income. Leisure time is included as having value and low crime rates and other factors, such as the cost of unemployment, the value of housework and education, and how the environment is impacted, are also evaluated. GPI attempts to measure the quality of life and not just economics.

The small Kingdom of Bhutan went even further, launching the Gross National Happiness Index (GNH) as the measure they would use to evaluate their political, economic, cultural, and environmental positions. The Nine Domains of GNH are: Psychological well-being (includes spirituality), Health, Time use, Education, Cultural diversity and resilience, Community vitality, Good governance, Ecological diversity and resilience, and Living standards.

In 2012, the Sustainable Development Solutions Network (SDSN), using data from Gallup, conducted its first annual World Happiness Report, building upon the concept in Bhutan to assess overall well-being. Switzerland, Iceland, Denmark, Norway, and Canada composed the top five countries in 2015.

On one side, were GDP and its friends: productivity, the merits of multitasking, and accessing the striatum, where new skills would be the key to lead us forward. An upward line of progression, just as the graphs reported. On the other, GPI and its friends: sustainability, focusing on single tasks, and accessing the hippocampus—recalling information.

No doubt 'experts' will argue for and against the merits of different models, but the graphs of GPI were not showing the climbing observed in GDP. Most reported drops, or at best, a flat line for quite some time. It was a close match to what I had seen in the decline of the usage of *progress* in written form. Coincidence? Perhaps, but we don't get out of bed each morning to chase productivity—we are in pursuit of happiness.

Learning new skills is a worthwhile endeavor, but to adapt to new places and environments we require spatial memory. This helps us to understand where we are now, how we got there, and how to reach the next destination. It's our road map and without it there isn't progress…we are lost.

As of 2015, 46.8 million people worldwide are living with dementia. A number predicted to double every 20 years. If global dementia care were a country, it would be the 18th largest economy in the world, exceeding the market values of companies such as Apple and Google.[14] Growing evidence links shrinkage in the brain, especially in one area, to an early warning of Alzheimer's disease, long before other symptoms appear. The affected area is the hippocampus—the same part of the brain that processes spatial memory.

A paradox was forming. As connectivity, the heart of the online world, grew stronger, links to certain areas in the brain were losing their grip. Despite the potential risks we have surged ahead. Pushed by web distractions and the increasing speed necessary to deliver on our multitasking outcomes, we are moving ever faster into a cave lit by neon bright lights we never imagine will be extinguished. To cope with the augmented communication channels, we no longer have time to pause and reflect, as new skills present themselves to be devoured. To contribute to this new connected world we have to be brief. We communicate in abbreviated text speak, tweet with 140 characters or less, and post our blog contributions as the 'five best...' or in bullet points, because it's all people have time to read and digest. Perhaps some of you stopped reading this essay 10 minutes ago because it's long. A variety of devices: laptops, tablets, phones, and watches, demand our attention, and provide some relief that we no longer need to trust only in our own judgment and can focus on the task of being more productive.

Behind this 'online curtain' is a world more troubling, which the wizard doesn't publicize on his web page. The very connectivity that requires our worship is pushing us into a blind allegiance to the technological supernatural. The very tools we so readily embrace have side effects—the reliance on spell check and calculators is dumbing down our ability to trust our own learning. GPS is creating a blind faith that it knows best, sending people driving into rivers and lakes, even when the obstacle is right before their eyes. Before GPS, we knew we couldn't cross a lake in a car without a bridge. Perhaps it's no surprise that research is beginning to demonstrate that excessive reliance on GPS is causing problems—where?—in the hippocampus.

And our children? We used to fear them falling from a bike or fending off a bully in the school playground, but that was in the old days (when I was a boy). Now, with no need for outdoor calming zones, they are tucked away at home behind closed doors, Skyping with friends they seldom see outside of school. It's there they encounter the world of digital predators and bullies who pursue their destructive agenda on social media. There, with controllers at the ready they learn how to be violent as adult counterparts sit in an office, using a joystick to direct drones to kill the declared guilty, along with the innocent. The 'collateral damage,' thousands of miles away.

Pursuing our connectivity deity, collecting our digital friends along the way, we are oblivious to the straight line thinking we support; just like GDP, driving the graph of electric impulses ever upwards. The paradox is laughing at us across the wires and web. The very basis of this new connectivity circuit is driving us to become aloof and disconnected from each other. Ever one click away from anonymous, we surf the 'net' to find the one app that satisfies our needs. Desensitized and without the boundary of real presence, we spew out our opinions without pause for reflection or impact.

No one talks about the future if the iCloud bursts and electrical impulses disappear. We should hope it happens soon, while there are still those among us who remember humanity before the World Wide Web and can lead the way, because the warning signs are beginning to emerge. More work time is not equating to increased productivity. Many workers, under pressure to perform and deliver are not taking their full annual leave entitlements and even those who do are unaware of the countless hours spent connected to work via handheld devices. Increasingly stressed, the effects, once again, are resulting in an opposite to the desired outcome, as productivity decreases and new health issues emerge. The young exhibiting emotional problems when WiFi is unavailable, is nothing compared to the possibility, as the hippocampus becomes unnecessary, within a few generations the brain chemistry of the new children will change—without a map to find their way.

It may sound like I am just technology bashing. An old fogie stuck in the past. The young might say I just have to get with the program, and perhaps you might say I should also focus on the good things we have accomplished. But does *progress* mean we are supposed to surrender our capabilities and destroy our well-being?

Perhaps subconsciously, we are aware. Despite the benefits, the deal we have made with the voltage God is not going to take us forward as much as we have been led to believe. It's why it hasn't been the spark to make us feel we are progressing upwards again. Although there have been huge gains in science and technology, there are echoes of parts of the past there has been no rush to change. I find it curious that we have retained such attachment to the internal combustion engine. When the landmark American civil rights legislation passed, taking 14 years of unbelievable struggle and loss to be accomplished, we might have expected the remaining walls of inequality to tumble. Yet, why are women still paid less than men for doing the same work? Perhaps women should start the long march to change, now.

I felt certain by only focusing on our current path we are chasing the wrong signal and the road map to what we are meant to be remembering and connecting to, in the depths of our hippocampus, is located somewhere in the past. Not back to 1993, when there were only 131 web sites (not the 700 million we have today); not to 1967, before the tumble began in '68, but aboard ship with Timothy the tortoise, as he journeyed back from the Crimean War in the 1850's.

The technical leap forward of the age, the industrial revolution, accelerated change to the same degree we experienced with the digital world over the last 20 years. What wasn't clear, were other changes creeping toward a conclusion as the 21st century approached. For thousands of years the mightiest had sought to spread power, control, and influence. The coming of the First World War was the 'war to end all wars,' but not in the way we imagined. The Greeks, Romans and many others had all faded and on the First World War battlefields the age of kings and empires ended for many. For the British Empire, what had been unthinkable fifty years earlier was now the slow death march into relative obscurity. Although it would still be many years before in sunk beneath the waves, the stubbornness to let go was overshadowed by a bigger question—what would replace Empire philosophy?

The signs appeared before the last shell exploded, as the Russian Bear discarded its Czars, and it continued, as autocrats in Spain, Italy, and Germany came to power. We had entered a new age of rival political philosophies, which all offered freedom from the bonds of the regal past—an end to the *Royal Progress*—the battle of the '*isms*' had begun. Communism, Fascism, Nazism, battled with propaganda, fear, and violence. As fortunes rose and fell, opposing sides in numerous conflicts fought for years as new '*isms*' joined the fray. Capitalism and socialism offered people different carrots and economic philosophies.

The constant changes and action kept everyone busy, with no time to consider that life in the age of kings may not have been perfect, but was easier to understand. We expected a monarch to be opulent, lavish, and rich. We knew the transfer of power through primogeniture was risky and getting a good one was a rarity we accepted. There was also no pretense about the wealthy. The King, Lords, Earls, and Dukes had the wealth—expected and out in the open, you were born into it, or not.

The new power was with the industrialists and bankers. As politicians aligned with big business, conflicts continued. The carrot was an *'ism'* that had to be defeated, but not included in the rhetoric, was a learning which many keep alive today. There was huge money to be made in wars for those with the right connections. War consolidates power for the winners and the generations of weapons provide an ongoing large income, through sales to the host government, 'friendly' governments, and other groups around the world.

In economies, it's a far more delicate balance and it's all about commodities, whether it's products, money, or people. Maximizing exports while providing cheap imports is highly desirable, especially for governments where up to 70% of the economy is based on consumer spending. Jobs and disposable income are critical components at home, as is locating a workforce abroad who can produce goods to import for low wages. Since the rich can always afford to buy, large populations of poor people are needed to produce the goods, with a steady group of middle earners available to do most of the spending. According to a recent report by the charity, Oxfam, the growth in the gap between rich and poor is growing at an ever faster rate. The world's 62 richest billionaires now own as much wealth as the poorer half of the world's population—about 3.8 billion people. It's the GDP of the wealthy on overdrive.

Moving toward the latest century, the world had changed much over the previous hundred years. For the most part, the voice of Fascism faded. Communism, once the great threat, hardly mentioned. The warring siblings, Capitalism and Socialism, continued to spat as always, but a gap formed, and for a short time a door opened to a different path. We didn't take it. We needed time and a leader to take us through, but the money wasn't right and the door slammed tight, by people who recognized the real power of '*isms.*' and the fears they can generate to keep the masses occupied.

Jingoism reappeared—the interference in foreign affairs. A philosophy driven by arrogance and superiority, which argued that protecting national security, decreed any action as valid. The 1950's 'reds under the beds' frenzy given life again as *terrorism* became the watchword, and the battle over religious models surged back from the past to claim innocent lives on all sides. The fog of war descended as friends and foes became lost in the mist.

One *'ism'* never materialized—*Peace-ism.* Leaders emerged to light the path, pursuing social change and freedom from the shackles of empire. They provided glimpses of what could be possible if we slowed down long enough to become learners and not sufferers. For peace is not about the absence of conflict. We need conflict—to be uncomfortable in our thoughts, ideas, and actions, so we can change. No, peace, is a process we use to resolve conflicts.

My visit to the past hundred years illustrated how everything has to fit into the models we pursue. Whether it's 'divide and conquer' economics, the fluidity of who are friends and enemies, which *'ism'* to battle or support, or how to resolve conflicts. We are often told the issues are complicated, but as I pondered...whatever solutions we choose—all have one critical question to answer—who benefits?

I don't believe most of us desire wealth and power and what we see in the GPI graphs and happiness scales are too many feelings of powerlessness and fear. Life will always be uncertain, but what we appear to be losing is our ability to slow down and reflect. As Mohandas Gandhi said, long before the Internet, "there is more to life than increasing its speed," and returning to the present I was left with an uncomfortable conclusion and a curious question. If we keep moving forward ever faster we won't notice the cost and what's not working. What if we could guarantee power and wealth to the same people who have it now, by choosing a path of peace? I must admit, I feel uncomfortable proposing it.

History has a long reach, but a short memory. We conclude and move on. I considered given up on my quest to locate a possible solution to our lost progress, when the dog reminds me it's time for her walk. Entering the calming zone around the corner, she pauses to sniff an interesting tree, when the local church bells chime. Then it hit me. Pulling the disgruntled hound back toward home, I am excited. Perhaps the *progress* problem is a spiritual disconnection, for God and spirituality don't exist in the '*isms.*' Memory...the hippocampus...could it be that simple, the reason for much of the discomfort was because we strayed too far from our spiritual home and the link, once strong, had grown weak?

I would have to go back further this time—long before 1856, to when God appeared, but when exactly was that? Judaism, Christianity, and Islam trace their origins to Abraham. They were inspiring times—the change from multiple Gods to the personal God. No longer banished to the sun, sky, and thunder, he was within us—in our hearts and minds. It should have been all we needed. We took this new God from the universe and gave him a home in glorious buildings we created, carved in stone and gold. He would be happy there; worshiped and adored. He would reveal to us the written word, which would light the path home. Then, it all went wrong.

We 'personalized' the personal God and created truth from his words. Truths which everyone needed to follow, whether they believed or not. Kings, Princes, and overlords fought and conquered and non-believers given the choice to convert or die. The various belief systems wrestled for hearts and minds and when internal quarrels flared, they separated into different factions, creating further reasons for persecution and death. Just like the '*isms*,' we always found the rationale to destroy, except this time the hypocrisy couldn't easily be hidden. It's difficult to be believed when one open palm offers the love, peace, and forgiveness of our chosen God, and the other, extreme violence, when you don't switch sides.

Creating religions hadn't delivered progress—I would continue the search. This time, back further, before the written word muddled minds—prior to self-serving Roman Emperors and Greek philosophers—to the Egyptians and the land of hieroglyphic symbols. They were an organized people and for Egyptians the real journey began after death, where 42 judges awaited them in the Hall of Judgment. A successful outcome led them to the Weighing of Heart ceremony, where good and bad deeds were examined, and if all went well, onto to heaven in the Field of Rushes. Life wasn't less complicated. With over 1,400 Gods and Goddesses, an Egyptian would have to pray to at least four a day just to keep up! Their beliefs provided structure, but *progress?*—I would have to look elsewhere.

It felt right to keep going back, but I hesitated. My 21st century brain cautioned a journey back further in time. *Progress*, it reminded me, was the modern world, not the past, but the more I had uncovered, the less confidant I felt the 'now' and all its speed could provide the answers.

Little is known about the distant past, but since the earliest times, I believe we have been searchers. Beginning with the daily quest for food, clothing, and shelter, our forbearers must have marveled at all they encountered. Perhaps, in a cave, long ago, flint or twigs created the first spark and the magic of fire was born. A eureka moment, which provided a sense of belonging and the impetus to consider the possibility of survival. The grunts and sounds no longer enough to express their observations and feelings, they needed a new magic. The first words slipping in unnoticed—a new name for themselves or the sun and moon sparkling in the sky.

Their discovery brought new power and a need to explain the forces behind the words. When the sun shone, they worshiped it; when the thunder boomed and lightning struck, they asked for forgiveness for perceived wrongdoing. With no modern distractions and immersed in nature, we can only wonder what Gods they created. They left few clues about their thoughts and beliefs, except for images, adorning the caves they inhabited, but what were they communicating?

The most common subjects were animals. Not surprising, given the role they had in providing the two necessities of food and clothing. With such importance, we would have to consider the possibility they saw animals as gifts from their Gods or even Gods themselves. In stark contrast to the detailed depictions of creatures, self-portraits are missing and pictures of people usually rendered as stick figures a three year old would draw. Did they see themselves as less significant and unattractive or did taboo have a part to play?

The other common theme was handprints, often drawn in clusters. An ancient artist's signature or just the easiest part of the body to draw around, it would appear there is little to go on, to illuminate the ancient world of our ancestors. The smelly ones we don't talk about at family gatherings. We can only speculate and before dismissing 'guessing' as having value, most of our concepts begin passage with a hypothesize, especially in our notion of a God.

In our journey thus far, we have observed part of what separates us humans from the other creatures who roam the earth, in our ability to develop new ideas, concepts, and understanding. Taking a fresh look at our cave dwellers, what might we uncover?

I am guessing you haven't been checking out cave drawings between updating your Facebook page and tweeting, but I encourage you to conduct a quick search. You don't have to be an artist to notice—they are really good! So? Maybe, they had nothing better to do after long day hunting or the men wanted to record a version of the great beast they killed. An ancient equivalent of a photograph of an angler holding his catch (less the distracting human). It's not what's there, but what's not there that bothered me. Where are the practice drawings? We know we need a huge number of hours to become good at anything, even for those with talent. Given the primitive tools at their disposal and a good chance, they may not have even had a language at the time; it seems unlikely and impractical they only kept the good ones.

There is more intrigue in the details of the pictures. Our prehistoric friends were not interested in still life interpretations. Most, show animals in motion and according to a study in PLOS ONE, conducted by researchers from Eotvos University in Budapest, Hungary, the skill of the artists is incredible. Most four-legged animals move their legs in a particular sequence and our cave dwellers accurately reported the correct order 53.8% of the time. It may not sound like a great success rate, until we conduct some comparisons. Since there are many potential combinations, guessing would result in a 26.7% chance of getting the gait correct. We can conclude, they didn't guess. Prior to 1880, great artists, including a famous horse picture by Leonardo da Vinci, yielded a mere 16.5%. In the 1880's scientists finally pinned down the sequence and we knew for sure which leg went before the other. Despite having this information, since 1887, only 42.1% of pictures and statues report the correct movement and even museum exhibits are not immune to error, with a 58.9% success rate in natural history museums.

Our ancestors were better observers and reporters. These hairy, prehistoric humans, to whom we give little thought or intelligence, could interpret the details of galloping animals. Unlike our modern fixation with speed and connection, they understood a link we have been struggling to hold onto.

The handprints provide further intrigue. Various explanations have been suggested for their inclusion. As we used our fingers to learn counting when we were children, perhaps they used the hands and fingers they drew on the wall as an ancient calculating system. Our hands are everything. A quarter of the part of the brain responsible for controlling movement is dedicated to hand muscles. They touch, feel, and act as transmitters of our emotions. Used in Christianity to invoke the Holy Spirit during solemn occasions and sacraments, in the ancient healing art of Reiki they help to balance the energies within the body.

We might imagine the men hunted the prey and painted the great animals on cave walls, adding their signature handprints. Like many assumptions, there is evidence to suggest otherwise. It's even a possibility that most of the handprints belonged to women, as the relative lengths of fingers are different between the sexes. Did men provide the food and women, as Shamans, the spiritual connection? We may never know, but before the written word appeared, language was born.

The journey of voice begins when a baby enters their eighth month in the womb, as their heart rate slows when their mother is speaking. It continues after birth, when they react differently when their mother reads a story compared with someone else. There is comfort, nurturing and peace in the tones of the heart, when shared with love. It may have been where it all began, as the men left to hunt; the women remained to nurture the little ones, forming the first words. As migration occurred, the era of yarns, tales and adventures traveled along. Unlike later, with words in books fought over for hundreds of years, the oral tradition offered something more magical—stories that could change with every telling, without loss of meaning and importance.

The real power of story is not in the reading, but in hearing the spoken word. When we engage our imagination and emotions, a transformation occurs within. As people scattered to far off lands and settled, I looked for other evidence they left to light our path. If they could paint more accurate pictures of animals in motion than we do today, what more might they have to share? I found it in the monuments they built—stone circles, which still mesmerize. With over 1,300 in Britain and Ireland alone, these were no whims. The most famous, Stonehenge, constructed over a 1,500-year period.

Experts continue to theorize on the their purpose: astrological guides, ancient Druidic temples, monuments to the dead? Whatever compelled the builders, constructing these sites required thousands upon thousands of hours and ancient engineering skills to transport and raise heavy stones. Without the written word, stories about these stones must have been handed down from one generation to the next—a narrative so powerful, people continued to build. Will the buildings we construct today have the same effect in a couple of thousand years? It's doubtful; because it's unlikely any will survive that long, because in contrast to our ancestors, we don't build to connect.

Earlier, I described the Latin root of *progress* as 'advancing or going forward,' but after my foray with Timothy to the 19th and 20th centuries and now in prehistory, I concluded, this definition is part of the problem, because it does not accurately describe positive change. When a circular ball rolls downs hill, we can say it progresses from the top to the bottom, but when it changes to an oval as it rolls, it does something else—it transforms. From the Latin, *transformare*, it literally means 'changing in shape,' and what lies at the heart of *progress* is a catalyst strong enough to make the change impactful and enduring.

Passion cannot be fleeting. When it is, we stop observing and reflecting. Our efforts of quick fixes, whether they are political, financial, or economical, fade and wither—we replace and not renew. We assume it's the hands of men who illuminate our darkness, when all along many handprints belonged to women—we continue to develop terrible weapons, but not to draw animals in motion correctly. We see GDP and view it, along with *progress* as wonderful upward lines stretching toward the sky, but what we have lost and need to recover is the wisdom of our ancestors. *Progress* is not about climbing graphs, but reaching to the heavens, by going full circle.

I am ready to get back to the present. I have a story to finish and for the first time in this journey, I realize in my search for truth and meaning, the answer has always been there, hidden in plain sight. It's not the conclusion I imagined when I started out with Timothy and it's not actually anything new at all. Perhaps, it is the only answer it could ever be; one which shows up everywhere—in night and day, hot and cold, sun and rain, in the seasons, light and shadow, but not in the *'isms,'* nor in any system that focuses on purely one outcome, whether it be a spiritual, political, economic, or environmental solution. The answer is balance, or more specifically, harmony. From the Greek, *harmonia*, it means 'agreement, concord of sounds,' and the echo of it reverberates from centuries past to the present time.

Part of me is sad to be back, but energized by my journey to the distant past, I feel a clarity emerging. Of all the discoveries, it's the workers who toiled at Stonehenge for 1,500 years, who are most on my mind. Such endurance, only possible because of connections to a story with its roots deeply imbedded in memory. We cannot afford to lose our hippocampus...to lose our way, because our ancestors are talking. They are pleading with us to reminisce, to remember the old days, when words became language; when language became song and our hearts touched the spiritual center that is the home of us all.

The light is dimming but it's not extinguished. We see it in how people with dementia become alive again when they hear poetry or music from their childhood. Within moments, a remarkable change occurs. Freed from the bounds of degenerative conditions, faces light up, the unspoken speak, toes tap, and hands clap as the music plays or the poem is remembered. People, who barely shuffle without music, glide across the dance floor as though the conditions they have no longer exist. Memories re-established, people become who they once were and the emotions return.

It makes perfect sense. When words were first recorded into writing they were not narrative accounts, rules, or laws, but great poems, such as Gilgamesh, Beowulf, and the biblical Psalms that spoke of stories and wisdom. One oral tradition handed down from one generation to the next through poetry, because just like music, lyrics we easily remember today, poems are much easier to memorize.

This is their message, handed down to us throughout time. To see the connection of stories, song and spirit, that unites, not divides, that touches us so deeply it can only heal when it is shared. The signs are there. Today, at life's most happy and sad moments we reach for the rhythm of our core to celebrate and mourn. At weddings, it's joyful singing, love poems and after dinner stories, we see as the way to express our happy feelings. At funerals, poetry is increasingly used to sing the words the heart is too wounded to speak.

Those who wish to rule continue to tell a story. It's their *Royal Progress,* kept alive by exploiting resources: labor, land, and assets, but the messages of our ancestors are not dead. The rhythm of life they imparted, found in those who blend the people, earth, and natural resources together in harmony. The 5,000 tribes, speaking 4,000 languages, who make up 5% of the world's population.

They are the indigenous people—First nations, the aboriginals; most connected to the cave artists. According to a study by Gonzalo Oviedo,[15] 80% of the global eco-regions (areas rich in bio-diversity, is inhabited by one or more indigenous peoples). There is a correlation between bio and cultural diversity. The people and the land, where resources are shared, not owned, where community lies at the center of their circle and where the Great Spirit speaks, because they actively seek to listen.

The response of the powerful to indigenous peoples across many nations throughout history has been disastrous. Lands seized and active policies enabled to destroy every facet of ancient cultures. Their languages forbidden, customs derided, forced to accept foreign clothes, schools, and Gods. Perhaps the worst atrocities were the efforts to destroy lives by infesting goodwill offerings with disease and introducing drugs like alcohol to cause dependency. Why would powerful forces go to such an extremes to exterminate whole peoples? The value of the land is a big motivator, but some actions seemed to go beyond mere natural resource seeking and wanting land for population expansion. It's as though they saw strength in these cultures beyond ancient ways and simple tools—societies blending body, spirit, land, in balance.

Our world has become a playground for the young, the fast and the furious, wrapped up in speed, with youthful leaders to match. Of US Presidents – John F. Kennedy, Bill Clinton, Barack Obama, three of youngest five ever at inauguration – British Prime Ministers – John Major, Tony Blair, David Cameron – also all their 40's. Populations are aging. Will we listen to our elders, tucked away in their nursing homes? We should, not only because of their wisdom, but soon they may be the only ones who can still remember what life was like before the memories died.

The search for identity and a God to identify with will always be our path. If we are in any doubt that it's native peoples we should be seeking to provide guidance and leadership, the commonalities in First Nations communities, separated by thousands of miles, is uncanny. Bright colors adorn their native dress. Music, dance, songs, tattoos and body paint mimic the beauty of nature and tell a story of who we really are...made in the image of our creator. They honor stories, the past, invoke their ancestors, and their elders are cared for and are the most respected in their communities. There are no coincidences...

For many in the western world we might appear very disconnected from this way of life, but in a strange way, the message is trying to get through. At sporting events we dress up, sing, paint our bodies, exude passion, and some say it's akin to a spiritual experience. We shouldn't be surprised. There are no coincidences...

We are all related and we were once all native peoples and can be again, when we reclaim the wisdom of the old ways. We need to transform and change shape back to the circle and the next time conflict is looming, let's not focus on argument or defend our positions. Perhaps all we need is a shared campfire, where we discover the rhythm that turns our spoken words to melodies and song into dance. It's there if we dare to believe in the force and power of story, we will see our ancestors, and know in truth and meaning we are all one people and the need for power and *'isms'* were just stories we chose to believe in.

An opportunity for a different choice is waiting around every corner. The greatest challenge we face is stubbornness. A willingness to give up our notions of success and consider the best answers to the future, maybe found in the distant past.

By 2018, dementia will become a trillion dollar disease. Natural resources continually depleted. Internet speeds ever faster. Our children disconnected. We can't just add these outcomes to GDP and say it's acceptable. The battle between fast and slow is one we must win. When we are unhurried, we provide the environment to connect with each other, where we encounter the magical kingdom of community—creating calming zones.

If Timothy had wisdom to share, he kept it to himself....for a very long time. By his death, as the United Kingdom's longest known resident in 2004, he had *progressed* to around 165 years old. As it turns out, we were as confused about Timothy as we are about our search to understand *progress*—it turns out, Timothy, was a girl.

FIVE

The Sandman

The Bible verses used in this essay are from The Jerusalem Bible, published in England in 1968 by Eyre and Spottiswoode. I chose this translation only because it was a gift from Mother when I was a child and I treasure it.

A boring lesson, an endless meeting, a brain starved of stimulation sends signals down the arm. Fingers twitch in response and reaching for a pen, pencil and a piece of paper, images begin to emerge. We may think of doodling as an innocent activity, lacking meaning; a way of passing time or processing frustrations and stress, but deep down in the recesses of our brains, we are problem solving.

We humans are a people of expression. Complex, deep thinkers, we are super creators, with a burning desire to explain ourselves and our world; through art, music, words, and even the approximately 17 muscles it takes to smile. We experience different states of consciousness, the unconscious, and in-between visionary conditions, which we often assume are an unconnected collection of thoughts, dreams, and desires. At one extreme is daydreaming, in which we almost fully remove ourselves from reality in short bursts. Flights of fancy we take on our own or in the presence of a loved one, but seldom in class or business meetings, where the risk of being singled out to answer a question remains a danger.

We need a different option—one with enough separation to process our thoughts, without the perils of total mental absence. Doodling is the perfect form and it has the additional benefit of potentially deceiving onlookers—we could just be taking notes! If you have doodled, you might stare at the results with the same disconnection you felt to the class or meeting that drove you to pick up the pen in the first place. What we draw most often are shapes and frequently we choose the same ones: stars, boxes, hearts, flowers, and writing our own name, occur with an eerie regularity. Perhaps we shouldn't be surprised. Carl Jung said, "Transformation takes place in the presence of images," and when look at all the great spiritual concepts—love, faith, hope, charity, and more, they are tools we are invited to use to lead on us on a path to change, because when we learn and grow, we begin in one place and end up in another. Unlike words, which mostly create certainty, images require interpretation, and it's within this space we encounter the possibility that solutions have more than one answer. Because images are muddled we are less likely to apply our greatest weapon of self-destruction—judgment.

In St. John's Gospel, there is a story, which scholars don't believe was authored by John. In it, Jesus delivers one of his many great one-liners to silence the Pharisees, who had a habit of being blinded by the word of the law, while ignoring its heart. The story of the adulterous woman[16] is striking because Jesus does something else other than listen and speak. "Master, this woman was caught in the very act of committing adultery, and Moses has ordered us in the law to condemn women like this to death by stoning. What have you to say? They asked him this as a test, looking for something to use against him. Jesus bent down and started writing on the ground with his finger." After delivering his superb retort, "If there is one of you who has not sinned, let him be the first to throw a stone at her," he bent down and wrote on the ground again.

Scholars have suggested several possibilities for what he might have drawn or written in the sand and although we can only speculate, none I am aware of suggested Jesus doodled. Perhaps we can't make the leap and prefer a theologically based answer to the sand mystery, as it fits better to images we feel we ought to have of the Son of God. Many had pushed his buttons for some time and he must have grown weary of the constant tests and weaknesses of humankind. We remember what happened to the money changers and we have other examples of his frustrations spilling over.

In the Gospel of Mark, a man appears with his son who exhibits epileptic like symptoms.[17] The man says, "I asked your disciples to cast it out and they were unable to." Jesus responds, "You faithless generation. How much longer must I be with you? How much longer must I put up with you?" As the boy's father asks for his help, Jesus reminds him, "Everything is possible for anyone who has faith."

Having faith is such a wonderful gift and truly, with it, everything is possible, but we often find ourselves challenged and troubled by the sands of time. We are the woman about to be stoned—judged and pronounced guilty, we feel powerless and alone. We are members of the crowd, ready to mete out justice, as we interpret it, to those we accuse. We are the questioned, by those who seek our support to justify their actions. We are the doodlers in search of a gospel that can change our view of others, ourselves, and make sense of our journey.

From the old English, 'Godspell,' Gospel is defined as 'good news' or 'glad tidings,' but 'spell' also has another meaning, as story, tale, or fable. Just as the biblical account reports the Gospel of Jesus, we too have our story to tell. Reading the accounts of his life, we may focus on the differences between us, but there are also similarities in our experiences. People question our words. We experience rejection when we speak or act and those we trust may betray us. We find it difficult to love our enemies and turn the other cheek as Jesus directed and our judgment is most fierce when applied to ourselves. We grow frustrated, stubborn, and stop seeing a way forward—we draw a line in the sand and struggle to budge.

Jesus preferred to instruct using parables. Accounting for almost a third of his teachings, and variously described as concise comparisons, analogies, illustrations and even riddles, they baffle their listeners. Used by countless educators, including Buddha and the great Greek Philosophers and present in all the major religious beliefs, they have almost disappeared in our modern world; lost to us. Why did the great spiritual masters choose parables to communicate? Why didn't they just say clearly what they meant? Actually, sometimes they did and so did

Jesus. When a man asked him what he must do to inherit eternal life[18] the man said he had kept the commandments, but went away sad, when Jesus told he should sell everything, give the money to the poor and follow him, because he was wealthy.

Hearing a straight-talking truth is difficult. We don't like being told what to do or think and tend to get defensive. They do serve to snap us out of the roadblocks we build to create space for the parables. These invite us to journey into the mystery the stories create, and because they are ambiguous, stimulate our curiosity and imagination to seek the truth they illustrate. We don't learn when given meaning. We must discover it for ourselves.

It's possible the mythical Sandman might sprinkle magical sand in our eyes at night, to give us dreams to show us the way, but it's more likely we will find our path by first 'shaking the dust from our feet,'[19] to rid ourselves of the illusion that we are innocent bystanders. It's what the stone throwers forgot when they approached Jesus with the law trap and although it's not recorded what was said as the crowd slowly dispersed, we can imagine, because we have all been there. 'The truth will make you free,'[20] and it will also make you extremely uncomfortable, which is the same blessing behind our doodling. A message is trying to make itself heard and it will try any means, including imagery and parables to grab our attention, because we have a gospel and glad tidings to discover and share in our own stories.

I can't imagine what the woman was thinking. There is a distinct lack of information in the text, which creates questions around her true identity. According to the Law of Moses, prior to stoning, she would have received a trial. It's curious that the Pharisees, so hot on the law, don't mention it. A trail, fair or not, would give them more solid ground for their argument, but they only say she was 'caught in the act.' Plucked off the streets as a pawn used by the Pharisees to corner Jesus, innocent or guilty as charged, her life must have flashed before her eyes.

Did Jesus doodle in the sand that day? I like to think so. I like to imagine he drew an image because he had a problem to solve. How to help us transform from enforcers of the law to ambassadors of forgiveness. How to help us see, in his story we can find our own and know the power of love is the *good news*.

SIX

The Butterfly Effect

Like all the best stories, it begins with…Once upon a time…but I am getting ahead of myself, because before thoughts of a story, there was a hunt to complete. How easy it is to misplace something and how difficult to find what is lost. We begin by looking in places that make the most sense; convinced we would have been thinking sensibly at the time we placed the item somewhere. When that fails, we turn to the next most logical location, until it turns into the grand search, and finally, when all else fails and frustration sets in…we plead. I am stuck and it's time for a quick prayer to St. Anthony, the patron saint of lost things in the hope he can help. 'Tony, Tony, look around, something's lost and must be found,' and then I am there…standing in front of the bookshelves.

Home to the most complex environment within our dwellings, they say more about us than any other location. Surrounded by dust with endless longevity, they contain so much more than books we expect to see. For many things without a home elsewhere, find their way to crowded shelves. Heaps of papers and photographs stacked on top of aging memories. Nick-knacks perched on the edges, ready to fall any time, and trophies hard won; reminders of a different age.

But, pride of place goes to the books. An assortment of wonders and wanderings, telling stories of past lives and un-kept promises—favorite recipes tucked inside guide books to places we visited or hoped to one day—a thesaurus and how to learn French in a week. Between the books is another world: letters written and forgotten long ago—postcards from relatives sending their love and wishing the rain would stop soon. Then there are the stories—perhaps romances, thrillers, coming of age tales, or biographies. Opening them, we remember and reminisce, keeping a favorite aside to read once again, hoping to be touched as deeply as we were once before. Clearing out some of the unwanted old, we make room for the new. It was at that moment, staring at an empty row, I pondered—if we filled the spaces we create with our own story, what would the shelf look like?

At first, the answer seemed obvious. Hasn't it been said before, that we all have our own book of life? Each chapter detailing the dramas, celebrations, disappointments, and joys of the different parts of our journey and how we would be very sure no one would be interested in reading it. Is life about writing our book and placing it on the empty space we create on our shelves?

There are plenty of views of what life is about. William Shakespeare thought of us as actors. "All the world's a stage and all the men and women merely players. They have their exits and their entrances."[21] Others say life is about art, music, or dance. Acting, painting, singing, making music? Perhaps, Forrest Gump's mother had it just right—"Life is like a box of chocolates," because it seems so often, we never know what we are going to get.

We are as fascinated with stories today as we have been since the beginning of time. Each takes us on a journey with someone to somewhere. We choose to go with them for many reasons, and when the last page is turned or the movie credits roll, we are satisfied. Glad we enjoyed it or happy it is over, we were touched and the memories of our experiences remain, calling out to us to visit again soon. So, do we place little importance on our own story, and if so, why?

We do. Constantly bombarded with images of success we feel the push to measure ourselves against the victorious. Judging how we look, what we have, and what we do, all contribute to pulling us further away from our essence, to a journey seldom satisfying. It is a diversion away from dissatisfaction and that's why it's attractive. Avoidance is also a productive tactic, because once we embrace it, we are able to make it self-perpetuating and it runs on its own without the need for intervention. Comparing, judging, and avoiding all contribute to our lack of interest in our life book, because if we write it under those conditions, we would have one chapter after another detailing how we measured down. The result, an extended resume filled with only the events of our lives and with a little creativity we can stretch it to several volumes, filling the space we cleared on our shelves. No wonder we wouldn't want it sitting there gathering dust, but comparing and avoiding are only distractions. To get at what's really occurring, we need to go back to our bookshelves; to the fiction books lined up side by side and ask a seemingly stupid question—what are they really about?

For example, a romance story—boy meets girl; loses girl; gets her back in the end, would appear to sum it up neatly, but we don't need 300 pages to describe three major events. We know that weaved between what happens, is the depth of the characters and how their choices, emotions, and dreams, connect them to each other, and if it's a great story—the relativity we see in own lives. There are millions of stories with more appearing each day. Billions of people, each with their own yarn to spin. How easy it is to feel overwhelmed and lose sight of our story on our journey, but help is at hand.

According to Christopher Booker in his book: "The Seven Basic Plots: Stories And Why We Tell Them," there are seven plots that cover all the stories we read: Overcoming the monster, Rags to riches, The quest, Voyage and return, Comedy, Tragedy, Rebirth. It's no coincidence that we experience all these story lines in some form on our journeys: overcoming fears, growth, seeking, humor, loss, and becoming, are all present. They all point to one major theme—change. Wanted or unwanted, change is a constant and if there were just one word to include in the title our life book it would be a strong contender.

We face obstacles along the path and make choices that decide how we make the journey, so what stops us from investing our total selves in this unique opportunity we have been given? It's more than our struggles with change...it's the lies and deceptions we speak in whispers, because we feel it's the safe road, which of course is another lie we discover later on. By that time, we have shut the door to change, found folly instead of wisdom, and can produce a list of reasons to prove the validity of our chosen approach. Despite all our resources: knowledge, facts, skills, experiences, and intelligence, they only help to provide us with an ample directory of excuses to support our lies. I call them the untruths of the shadow, because once we embrace and feed them, they never leave our side, driving us far away from our story.

I can't...I have listed this one first as it's the showstopper. When we employ this approach, we are left stuck at the starting line with no drive to move forward. Since the depletion of energy we feel by saying, 'I can't,' deprives us of the resources we are going to need to finish the race, this stubborn habit requires two steps to overcome. The first is to stop deciding what outcomes need to look like. Every 'I can't' contains a pre-determined future, which we fill with unhappy endings. Removing it creates room for *all* the possibilities. Our minds will push to fill this space with logic, firing up the reasoning part of the brain in an effort to convince us with rational thinking to abandon the quest. Trust your intuition and move forward—"If you think you can...or if you think you can't...you're right."[22]

I have nothing new to contribute...How much we do embrace our uniqueness? Don't diminish your journey as being insignificant because you have been called here by name. Think of the books on your shelves—there are only so many words and ways to combine them, yet it doesn't stop us from wanting to read, does it? When you were born, a new soul was summoned here to accomplish something. Seek it for it is for you alone—don't ask for permission, nor seek approval. Your words and actions are for your unique story.

I don't fit in with what the world wants...
Indoctrination is pervasive in our societies. Our schools lay out a required path to the work future. Our workplaces, necessary steps to success. Our media, what beautiful looks like. How do feelings of not smart enough, successful enough, and attractive enough, support your journey? This is not our home. We are visitors here and when we are away from home, do we not seek what gives us joy and happiness? We don't ask the world to decide. Being in the world doesn't mean we have to be of the world, and just because there are powerful messages in the shadows, it doesn't make them right or truth. Ignore those voices and follow the one that speaks inside of you.

I am not creative...At first glance, you may think this an odd choice, but how often do we compare the gifts of others to what we see in ourselves? The great violinist, artist, thinker, or winning idea. We fall short and the comparison limits us to seeking what we have been given. We see gifts as the world defines them and rate them as society says they have value—in the riches of possessions and wealth of money. We say, 'if I can't be that good, why should I bother, because someone is always better.' Creativity is not about a human end, but a spiritual process; where the connection opens a channel to the true treasures; given to support your journey, and in doing so, the journey of others. Before creativity is doing, it's being, and when we create space, we open the door to the greatest creations—love, forgiveness, kindness, and compassion. "Creativity is not the finding of a thing, but the making something out of it after it is found."[23]

I have no purpose...You are the narrator and protagonist of the only story that matters—yours. There is something you need that you don't have, and your story, your purpose, is to find it—with every step; every breath. You must trust that it will be revealed to you, so listen and watch for the signs. No matter what anyone says, don't expect it at a particular time or under certain conditions. People will cross your path. Some will be a blessing you will embrace and others, lessons you will want to push away. Accept all you encounter and take time for self-reflection, not judgment. Embrace change, for without it we are stuck in the land of shadows, and when all seems lost and forsaken, ask for guidance in the quiet stillness. It will come on gentle breezes and in quiet whispers, holding you close and asking for your trust.

The Butterfly Effect

The moment we agree to a lie our mind finds every reason to support it. That's why our answers can't be found in the ego and they have to be elsewhere. We call the place many names: heart, heaven, soul, spirit, light, love. Whatever is right for you, name it, and go there every day to banish fear from your story, because it's never been 'us against them.' It's us against ourselves. Like the butterfly who as an egg, pupa, or caterpillar cannot see where its future will be, we must trust our path and our story.

Standing before my bookcase, I feel better about placing my life book on the shelf, but is embracing change and banishing lies enough to make my 'one upon time story' the best it can be, because who puts only one book on an empty shelf? We fill up the space, and in thinking about which other books should keep my life book company, I realized that to become the butterfly we all desire to be, we need something more, because butterflies don't just change—they transform.

The Greek word for butterfly is 'psyche,' which is also the same word for 'soul.' It's not a coincidence and neither should be the other books we place on our empty shelf. They need to be what feeds our story— what supports and encourages the transformations throughout our lives—they need to be our reference books. In, are the books on kindness, compassion, forgiveness, and healing. Out, are books on regrets, fears, guilt, and the past.

To...not want our lives to be about change, but transformation. To...remember, for all their beauty, a butterfly cannot see their own wings, but they share their splendor with us without knowing, as we must do for each other, even when we don't see our own beauty.

If you are feeling uncomfortable, it might be time for a trip. There's no need to pack. In fact, before you go, unpack all your worries, fears, and conditions. Go to the most important room where you live—it's the one where a bookcase is waiting. It's time to review what you have; to clear a shelf for you reference books. The ones needed to lead you to transforming your 'once upon a time' story. So, embrace The Butterfly Effect, where one change in the complexity of your being, sends the beauty of your soul soaring out to the world.

Seven

The Special Theory of Spiritual Relativity

Summoned to the Headmaster's office, I approached with anticipation. The secretary said he would be back in a couple of minutes and I should go in and wait. On entering, another person also waited. Looking up from his chair, an old man with a huge grin, filling his whole face, asked, "Are you intelligent?"

An unexpected question, I fumbled for an appropriate answer. Should I lie or tell the truth? I had to decide, and fast. "I don't know," trickled out of my mouth. It seemed like the best choice; hardly convincing, but not really saying anything at all. I didn't know then. The smartest thing to do would be to answer his question with a question. That would have been very smart, but I wasn't smart. He said nothing, grinned again, and as the Headmaster returned, the uncomfortable moment passed.

The man had come to give us a presentation and I was to show him to the school hall to prepare. I don't remember the details of what he talked about, nor his specific words, but I do remember how it made me feel. How he spoke painted a picture which I could see clearly—it was magical and at the time I thought it must be what intelligence truly is—I was 11 years old.

From the moment we take our first breath, we are thrust into a world of learning. Our parents are our first guides. They show us what's good to touch and chew, watching over us with love and care so we don't come to harm. They pass on their feelings, beliefs, rules, and behaviors. We rely on them to provide expertise so we can navigate through this strange place we have found ourselves. We believe what we are told because we don't have enough information to consider other answers.

When we arrive at school a new set of experts instruct in other areas we know nothing about. There are mathematical problems to solve, languages to learn, history to review, and...a new set of rules to follow. We believe what we are told is important, most of the time, because we don't have enough information to consider other answers.

I struggled through school. I didn't feel stupid, but most subjects seemed beyond my grasp and good results were rare. As the school years passed I wanted to understand why—why my friends did so much better—why Spanish, Latin, physics, and mathematics all felt like foreign languages and why I needed extra mathematic lessons outside school to help me understand equations, algebra, and Pythagoras's theory. Perhaps I didn't have any Greek blood in my veins or lost out in the gene pool lottery. I had kept all my old school reports from Primary school onwards for years and spent an evening sifting through them trying to find answers. There it was...clearly stated time and time again by one teacher after another. There was one thing I was very good at—being 'conscientious.'

Excited, I wanted to rush into school to ask the Headmaster when the 'conscientious' class would begin and how I expected to do so well. I was sure he would be thrilled I had finally discovered my place in the school world and it was just possible I could come top. No promises...but there was a chance. There was only one problem. Teachers spent all day imparting knowledge and my job as a student was to learn and repeat it back through tests, tasks, and verbally answering annoying questions in class. It was not enough just to keep trying. Success at school had an expiration date. I pictured the old man with the huge grin, sitting in the Headmaster's office, asking me again if I was intelligent—'No, I am not,' I would have to say, because experts provided the rules and the definition, and no matter what I thought, I didn't have enough information to provide another answer.

On April 18, 1955, Albert Einstein died in Princeton hospital. Somewhat controversially, but understandably, his brain was removed. A maverick genius, if there was a brain worth studying from the past hundred years, it would be his. If his brain had been larger than others it would have been a straight forward conclusion to account for his uncanny abilities, but it wasn't. Despite numerous examinations over the years, the experts have disagreed on what they see. The 'relativity' they seek, between his brain and what he achieved, remains elusive; hidden behind a veil of possibilities and unproven connections. What if the link between intelligence and relativity relied on more than pure brain power and what if Einstein's greatest gift to us was not the discovery of specific relationships in his scientific findings, but how he got there?

Our lives beyond school lead for further encounters with experts. Wherever we go, there are voices telling us more about our subject, profession, and expectations. We instinctively trust some more than others and according to a worldwide "Trust in

Professions 2015" study,[24] trusted professions include nurses, doctors, and teachers.

People don't always come out and say they are experts, and although Franklin Roosevelt said, "there are as many opinions as there are experts," we consciously and sometimes, subconsciously, decide who to listen to and why. Position, education, practice, trust, and previous experience all play their part and we may believe they found their path through talent, hard work, insight, and maybe, a little luck.

Politicians score very low on the trust scale. Running for office, they tout their abilities to fix things and make the economy and our lives better. They describe their skills, achievements, and experience—in short, they sell themselves as experts. Once World War II ended, the crying of babies was heard around the world, as what became known as the 'baby boom' exploded. Lasting until 1964, it created 76 million new lives in the USA alone. It doesn't take a mathematical genius (or me) to figure out there would be a huge increase in the number of retirees 65 to 80 years later. Along with longer life expectancy, increases in medical and living needs for elderly care and higher outgoings for social security retirement payments, it doesn't take a rocket scientist to realize it would create severe economic challenges. Yet despite all the time, all the experts, and all the opportunities, many countries are not only still very unprepared, they are operating under huge amounts of national debt—fiscally bankrupt. Expertise is more than facts and figures.

Struggling to connect knowledge and expertise with intelligence, I opened the dictionary. Intelligence derives from the Latin verb, *intelligere,* the ability to think, to comprehend or perceive. It wasn't the definition I expected. Rather than providing clarity, it said nothing about applying intelligence. We all think and create perceptions, but we don't all change the world with our findings, so how did Einstein do it and why should it matter?—after all, I failed physics, quite badly by the way.

In 1905, he published his paper on Special relativity. His insight – Two events that appear to be simultaneous to one observer will not appear to be simultaneous to another observer who is moving rapidly. And there is no way to declare that one of the observers is really correct. Ten years later, he published his generalized theory, providing the equations that show: gravity, time, space, energy, and acceleration are all related.

It's amazing stuff and my brain still struggles to process all its meaning. It's not because I don't have much of a science brain, which I don't, but because unlike Einstein, I spent too many years believing in the authority of experts, which he constantly questioned and too long looking for concrete answers, rather than trusting in my intuition.

His observations have had a huge impact on our world, from the development of things we use every day of our lives to understanding the cosmos and it's an event from his early life that led me down a path, far away from physics and mathematics. Seeing a compass as a child gave him insight, that there are invisible forces guiding the universe, with rules that could be discovered and understood. Because, deep rooted in all our lives are answers to other questions we feel the need to pursue. Links to other invisible forces. Einstein may have wondered what it would be like to ride at the speed of light alongside a light beam, whereas most of us have different questions. Why are we here? Where did we come from? Where are we going when we leave? Who created us? Is it possible Einstein illuminated another path— one that could lead us to a theory of spiritual relativity?

History and the present, has given us many spiritual guides: Buddha, Jesus, Mohammed and many others. We don't use the word expert to describe them. We use: the Awakened One, Teacher, Prophet and we continue to talk about them hundreds of years after they died because they touch in us something deep inside—questions we want to answer. Their words and actions help us to consider different possibilities, offering guidance on various paths to follow. They share commonalities that very much fit the list of trusted professions—caring, loving, healing, and learning, and perhaps the greatest gift we have been given is the free will to choose the way that's right for us. It may or may not following the teachings of one of the few I listed, because we are a world full of uniqueness—of different races, colors, and cultures, speaking 6,500 languages—one of 8.7 million species inhabiting the earth.

It would appear that the God or Creator of our understanding has created a variety and richness in our world, and would be pleased that we choose to undertake a spiritual journey at all, rather than decide only one way is correct. Many spiritual experts have appeared over the years. Some have added to the light of their guides, but others have used beliefs as a weapon and created rules and structures which must be followed. How teachings have been interpreted lies at the heart of much of the discord that has followed. Insistence that only one path is correct blinds us to the beauty found in all. Just as it would foolish to be immersed in nature and judge each flower and tree for being different. They are all beautiful.

Einstein faced a similar crossroads in his world of physics. His theories pushing against the status quo of commonly held beliefs of his contemporaries. Worse, just as we encounter the different versions of God in various belief systems, he had to face his own

The Special Theory of Spiritual Relativity

nemesis, who although long since dead, held power in the court of physics, mathematics, and astronomy—Sir Isaac Newton. It was Newton's laws of motion and universal gravitation that shaped the fundamental principles of understanding the invisible forces that fascinated Einstein. Taking on Newton and his fellow physicists would be akin to saying religious belief systems were all missing something important about spirituality that makes all the difference.

In a quest to develop a Theory of Spiritual Relativity caution is needed. Although Einstein is viewed as a radical thinker, who shook up the physics world, his theories were securely based on the work previously done by others. Ours should be the same, for there is so much we have learned from the great spiritual teachers about love, faith, hope, and trust. At its core, Einstein's gift to the world was defining the link between various elements—unlocking the mysteries about space and time and proving their relationship.

We have our own mystery to solve. It also revolves around invisible connections and a desire for understanding and growing our relationship with our creator. We feel forces around us—in nature—and inside us—in our spirit or soul, and if "Genius is the fusion of an adult's rational will with the innocent perceptions of a child,"[25] Einstein gave us a place to start. We expect the great ones to have intellects the size of elephants and certainly Einstein was not a slouch in that department, but he valued other concepts, which included "intuition, inspiration, and imagination," ranking the last above abilities we would normally associate with very smart successful people.

It didn't sound very scientific. He was known for his Gedankenexperiments (thought experiments) and I needed to test out his statement on imagination using something similar. I knew I couldn't think like him, but my own intuition led me to the novel I was working on. In the story, there is scene where the young protagonist opens a last letter from his best friend, whose grave he stands beside. It's a highly-charged emotional few minutes and is important it conveys all the pain, fear, and despair he feels. I read through my written words, closed my eyes, and pictured the scene. It was unnerving as it unraveled before me, just like watching a movie on a big screen. It would have been easy to dismiss it as purely a rendition of what I had written, but, my words had focused on the emotion and had little detail about the actual scene location. Somehow, my brain had instantly built all of it...in detail—what the cemetery looked like; the trees; the bridge; the river. Even the weather.

Imagination is not frivolous daydreaming and by touching the emotional heart, everything else fell into place. It was, perhaps, a small window to what Einstein experienced and I wondered, if we were able to imagine how much we are loved, what it might change in us and in our world. How much do we listen to others who tell us we are wrong? How often do we embrace the thoughts of experts? How frequently do we convince ourselves we are not smart enough? But, love, faith, hope, and trust have no need for experts—only our willingness to connect to our spiritual center and be open to what happens next. With acceptance of the possibilities, who knows what missing details will be revealed.

Interestingly Einstein didn't see himself as being particularly talented. Most would disagree, but we have to ask, why did he discover a new theory and not his contemporaries? There were some very capable physicists at that time, but many were not so willing to give up the previous conclusions of others or themselves. How often do we cling onto old thoughts and ideas? How often do they stop us from moving forward? Being open to change lets the new, enter. When we say, 'I don't know,' we give permission for a spark to start a new fire of discovery in ourselves. Einstein peeled away the layers of complexity which he saw as barriers to understanding. Looking at every problem simply, cleared his mind of unnecessary clutter.

In our spiritual lives we can benefit from doing the same. We place so much between us and our God, it's no wonder it's a struggle to feel the full light of love that's offered. The more time we give to fighting over whose version is correct; the more time we spend in judging and not accepting; the more time we decide what is a sin and what is not—it's all wasted time.

With his endless curiosity, Einstein added another powerful supporter in his search to find answers. Both curious and cure have their roots in the Latin word, 'cura'—care. Perhaps it's another reminder. An echo of what we value in trusted professions, nurses and doctors—what we can achieve when we care for each other, ourselves, and our spiritual journey.

There comes a time when the outward focus on life, work, family, and career, turn in a new direction. It's this inward glance that opens a creaking door to a sleeping mystery, bringing a desire to be alone in a place, lacking the teaching voices or rules, imposed. Nature summons us to her court of non-judgmental beauty, where thoughts find meaning and the quiet speaks until we listen. Maybe, it was when sailing his boat, the final pieces of his theory of relativity fell into place or in a melody, he played on his violin, which created another path to the mystery.

We don't have to find all our answers and nor should we try, because complication is the enemy of simplicity, but now and again they come our way, as a reminder that holding onto the past doesn't serve us well; when we allow experts or ourselves to be convinced of truths we label as knowledge. My elderly mother loves to reminisce. On a recent visit, she described how she used to help at my primary school, but wasn't always popular with the Headmistress with her forward thinking ideas. Then it slipped out. "I wasn't happy that you missed a year of mathematics, because the teacher forgot to teach it," she said. I had no recollection of it. How long I had believed it was all a lacking in me causing my problems with numbers. A few months before, I had another one of those moments. Reading, while my wife sat next to me studying a text book, I asked her what she was doing. She explained she was starting a 3-step process: "First I highlight, then, I make notes in the margin, and for the last step I write a summary." I asked her why she does it that way. "Because it's how I learn," she said. It hit me right away. One of those aha moments—all those years at school and no one taught me how to learn. I just didn't know how and still don't.

In 1983, alas, after I finished school, American developmental psychologist, Howard Gardener, theorized 9 types of intelligence. No doubt, there will be other experts who may disagree. As for me, I am happy with my 'conscientious.' I smile that its roots lie in 'conscience'—which means, 'with knowledge.' I forgot my school education long ago and as the years pass, I embrace all I can learn. I may not have got better at learning complex things, but in practicing simple acts of forgiveness, kindness, and compassion, I feel the simplicity of our call to love with all our passion filling me completely.

A question still remains. Is there a Special Theory of Spiritual Relatively? I don't think so. I believe there are many, because we are all unique: all special. Einstein was on a constant mission to seek unifying theories and this is my unifying theory for all of us—the human race—so much more alike than we are different. The theory is based upon the following principles:

- The principle of spiritual relativity: The laws of love don't change, even for people moving at variable speeds in different spiritual directions
- The principle of the power of love: The power of love has the same value for all observers regardless of their motion relative to the love source, without the need for uniform agreement on where the love comes from
- Love is constant, but relative. The faster we move toward it, the slower time passes and the ability to love, increases

- According to the Theory of Spiritual Relativity when we are open to giving and receiving love, with kindness and compassion and without judgment, we are *all* right—we all belong here; no exceptions

It's a beautiful day. I can't play the violin; I don't have a boat to sail, but mounting my bike, it's not Einstein's words, but Mark Twain's that come to mind - "You can't depend on your eyes when your imagination is out of focus." Leaving home, I wonder if that's the key. Seeking balance brings everything we need in our lives, in the right measures at the right time. Balancing all our 'I's:' Intelligence, intellect, intuition, inspiration, and imagination opens us up to all the possibilities. Within moments, I am through the park and down at the water's edge, pausing by a sign showing a man with sparkling eyes and crazy hair. It says, from 1922 (when he was 43 years old), Albert Einstein rented a small summer cottage nearby.

Dismounting my bike, if I look very hard...I see him outside, puffing on his pipe and scribbling theories on a sunny day. His success before reaching 40, not matched again in the years to follow. I wonder if it's crossed his mind, that much of his ability to find a new path was because he was so skeptical of authority—after all his success, he was the authority now.

If he were sitting there, would I have the courage to approach? In the past, with my little understanding of mathematical formulas or theoretical physics, I doubt there would be much to discuss, but it's different now, because I am getting better at imagining. I still have lots to learn. I think he might tell me—'I found the path before my contemporaries, because they held onto beliefs and rules others had taught, and I didn't.' Life is not about clinging onto old ideas that either experts or we have pronounced as truths, but seeing with fresh eyes when the light of love illuminates our hearts and minds.

I wonder...what if he looked up with his big smile and asked, "Are you intelligent?" I would tell him that I see things differently now, because I have enough information to consider other answers. I might share with him that scientists rated quite well in the list of most trusted professions. I am sure he would find it amusing. I would tell him the most trusted profession across the world are not nurses, doctors, or teachers, but firefighters, because not only do they care for us and our possessions, but risk their own lives to do so. I might tell him, the word 'genius' is Latin (which he probably already knows) and that it means, a guardian deity or spirit which watches over each person from birth.

Einstein found the key to the problem of relativity using time, and as I examine my journey time, it's just possible I have believed too much what others told me...and the story I told myself...because I was taught to follow the rules and listen to the experts. It's there, in those early years, I remember...no one taught me how to walk or eat. It's there, in the young years, I remember...no one taught me how to smile and laugh. It's there, in the growing years, I remember...no one taught me how to cry and dream. It's there...now...and although we may sometimes seek the counsel of others, it's not to get their answer, but to help us discover our own, dwelling within. For others see us in pieces and not the whole. They may see the shadow and not the soul. They make up their minds of who we are, but they don't have enough information to truly understand. For although we may be alike, in each breath we take, our thoughts, feelings, emotions, and beliefs combine in uniqueness, and I realize that each of us is an expert after all...on ourselves and our own spiritual journey.

Like Einstein, our answers are found in time, and the journey truly begins when the outward focus no longer satisfies and we take the path inside, because it's our relativity we seek. So, "be yourself; everyone else is already taken,"[26] and realize, we truly have all the information we need to find our answers. Staying curious and scribbling in our notebooks on a summer's day...to recognize our expertise and let it be our guide—to fight our fires and risk all with passion, to discover our own unique spiritual path. Our one of a kind, Special Theory of Spiritual Relativity.

About the Author

Born and raised in London, England, Francis worked as a missionary, living and working with the poor and homeless in the United States. His non-fiction presents thought-provoking insights into the mystical journey of life and his fictional writing bring together a unique blend of history and spiritual storytelling in the style of parables, where he encourages readers to find their truths hidden in plain sight. He lives in Berlin, Germany with his family and when he is not writing, he attempts to share the mysteries of life with his dog—with little success.

I hope you enjoyed reading this book and feel inspired to further adventures. Word-of-mouth is crucial for any author to succeed, so I would greatly appreciate your support by leaving a review on Amazon and your favorite book websites, if you have time. Even if it's only a line or two, it would be a huge help—thank you.

If you would like to get an automated email when Francis's next book is released and/or receive an occasional newsletter, visit francisjshaw.com (francisjshaw.com/free-goodies-2/stepping-stones-newsletter/). Your address will never be shared and you can unsubscribe at any time.

You are most welcome to follow Francis's inspirational posts on Facebook (facebook.com/FrancisJTShaw)

Francis can be reached by email at francisjshaw.com

Feeling stuck and need direction? Check out your soul stones by clicking on the **Stepping Stones** button at francisjshaw.com

Endnotes

Breadcrumbs

[1] Victor Hugo

[2] Dietrich Bonhoeffer

The King's Gambit

[3] Benjamin Franklin, The Morals of Chess, (1750)

[4] Fourth Lateran Council, Canon 68

[5] Published in 'The Week in Chess.'

[6] The Way of Perfection, St. Teresa of Avila

[7] Schach ohne Partner für Könner by Herbert Grasemann (1982)

Progress and Timothy the Tortoise

[8] William Blake. *Jerusalem.*(1804)

[9] Alfred, Lord Tennyson, Charge of the Light Brigade (1854)

[10] William Blake. *Jerusalem.*(1804)

[11] Google Books Ngram Viewer search for *progress* (results include all English usage, wherever English is spoken)

[12] Cited in Cook, E. T. The Life of Florence Nightingale. (1913) Vol 1, p 237

[13] Stanislaw J. Lec

[14] Alzheimer's Disease International, World Alzheimer Report (2015)

[15] World Wildlife Fund, (2000)

The Sandman

[16] Gospel of St. John 8: 1-11

[17] Gospel of St. Mark 9: 14-29

[18] Gospel of St. Mark 10: 17-22

[19] Gospel of St. Luke 9:5

[20] Gospel of St. John 8:32

The Butterfly Effect

[21] 'As You Like It'

[22] Henry Ford

[23] James Russell Lowell

The Special Theory of Spiritual Relativity

[24] Carried out by GfK Verein, in which more than 29,000 consumers were surveyed. People from 27 countries around the world were interviewed with the aim of discovering the level of trust they have in 32 pre-determined occupations

[25] Charles Baudelaire

[26] Oscar Wilde

Printed in Great Britain
by Amazon